SOLD! BY OWNER

LYNN LARABIE

PRENTICE-HALL CANADA, INC., SCARBOROUGH, ONTARIO

ISBN 0-13-826199-7

0 57812 26199 0

Canadian Cataloguing in Publication Data

Larabie, Lynn
Sold! by owner

ISBN 0-13-826199-7

1. House selling. I. Title.

HD1379.L37 1990 333.33'8 C89-090790-0

Prentice-Hall Inc., *Englewood Cliffs, New Jersey*
Prentice-Hall International, Inc., *London*
Prentice-Hall of Australia, Pty., *Sydney*
Prentice-Hall of India Pvt., Ltd., *New Delhi*
Prentice-Hall of Japan, Inc., *Tokyo*
Prentice-Hall of Southeast Asia (Pte.) Ltd., *Singapore*
Editora Prentice-Hall do Brasil Ltda., *Rio de Janeiro*
Prentice-Hall Hispanoamericana, S.A., *Mexico*

Production Editor: William Booth
Cover: Blake Foy
Manufacturing Buyer: Luca Di Nicola
Composition: CompuScreen Typesetting Ltd.

ISBN: 0-13-826199-7

Printed and bound in Canada by Webcom

1 2 3 4 5 W 94 93 92 91 90

TABLE OF CONTENTS

INTRODUCTION

I sold my own house. I'm not a real-estate agent, nor have I ever been involved in the real-estate business. The house I owned had been purchased through an agent. Prior to the selling of my own home, I had neither experience nor knowledge in this field.

Originally, I had no intention of selling my own house. I was a "retiring" military doctor. I had planned on going the traditional route, by hiring a real-estate agent. Unfortunately (or fortunately), the terms of my military contract did not include any costs associated with selling the house. My house was in a small Saskatchewan town, considered to be a buyers' market, with a low annual increase on the selling price of homes (3%). Since I had owned the house for less than three years, I realized that the 6% real-estate commission would be a staggering amount of money. I considered the amount I had invested in renovating the home and what would remain after the realty fee had been subtracted. In order to break even on the sale of my house, I would have to do it on my own.

A surprising thing happened. Once I had begun to nurture the idea of selling the house myself, it became a challenge. If I can sell my house, you can do the same.

As with most do-it-yourself projects, I needed information to get started. I knew what I had paid for the house, and a few of the facts, but that was about it. To get more in touch with my home, I compiled all available documentation about the house — mortgage papers, offer to purchase, and surveyor's certificate.

Just how do you go about selling your home? After all, it must be quite complicated if many people earn a living selling houses. I went to several stores and libraries, hunting for information, and was amazed at the scarcity of books on the subject.

I memorized every available pearl of knowledge and craved more. I talked with people who had sold their own homes. (By the way, they're hard to find, but gradually increasing in number.) I was fascinated by the planning and selling process, and every new piece of information helped me to gain the confidence to try it on my own.

My experience gave me many insights on how to successfully sell your home, which I would like to share with you. I believe a perspective from a person without formal real-estate training is invaluable. It proves that anyone, *regardless of background*, can sell his or her own home.

It's your home. No one can represent it as well as you can. You love the place. You're proud of it. You've lived in it and with it for years. You don't have to be part of the background, as some real-estate agents would have you believe.

In this age of inflation, selling your own home is a good way to earn thousands of dollars. To forfeit a substantial margin of profit by hiring someone else to sell the house is a pitiful waste.

You may even get a better price for your home if you sell it yourself. To stay in business, a real-estate agent has to sell several homes concurrently. The average realty commission is 6% of the total selling price of the home. Suppose you would like to sell your home for $187,000, and the real-estate agent would like you to list it for $184,000. What's 6% of $187,000, compared to $184,000? Not much. It's a difference of $180 to the real-estate agent, but it's $3000 to you, plus the $11,040 for the luxury of having the house sold for you.

The higher the asking price of the house, the more work it is to sell. What real-estate agent would be willing to spend an extra month or two trying to sell at your price of $187,000, when all he or she stands to gain from the effort is an extra $180? No one can blame the agent. Rather than admit this, some agents will try to convince you that your house is worth only $184,000. They will mention that nicer homes in your neighbourhood have sold for less than the price you want. They'll warn you of the pitfalls of over-pricing yourself and losing potential buyers. They'll remind you of the amount you originally paid for the house, and use this figure to convince you that you're making a fair profit. I know this is true because it happened to me.

The lesson to be learned from all this? Trust yourself. Don't ever believe that a real-estate agent can get you a better deal for your house than you can get on your own. You have a 6% realty-fee saving with which to bargain. Most people who are interested in buying your house will realize this, and it will be your ace in the hole.

You don't need to be reminded how much of your income goes to taxes. Capital gains acquired from selling a primary residence are tax-free. The amount you will save by selling the house on your own is also tax-free. For example, using 6% as the average brokerage fee, if you sell you home for $187,000, you forfeit $11,220 of profit to the agent. Think about how long you would have to work to save $11,220 tax-free dollars. Don't you think selling your own house is an option worth serious consideration?

Aside from financial gains, few experiences match the satisfaction and sense of accomplishment of selling your own house. You feel like you can take on the world. I know I did.

CHAPTER 1

WHY PEOPLE DON'T SELL THEIR OWN HOMES

Why are you selling your present home? Do you have to relocate because of occupational requirements? Has your family outgrown the size of your current home? Are you retiring and wish to have something smaller with less maintenance? Or, do the disadvantages of owning your present house outweigh the advantages?

Regardless of your reason for selling, if you have enjoyed your home, someone else will, too. Unless you don't have time, there's no good reason why you can't sell it yourself.

If selling a house without a real-estate agent is such a great idea, why doesn't everyone do it?

MENTAL SET

For many years it has been customary to hire a real-estate agent to sell your home. How did this tradition originate? Think of a time when people travelled by horse and buggy. Villagers got together and built their homes, and most lived out their lives in one place. They traded or sold their goods to each other, and enjoyed a self-sustaining community life. Occasionally, families would have to move elsewhere. Not many homes were up for sale. In addition, communication was slow and unreliable. Looking for a home miles away (and worlds away) posed a difficult challenge.

Thus, the first real-estate company came into existence. For a modest fee, the real-estate agent brought together buyer and seller.

What has happened in the 90s? We have become a mobile, fast-moving society. Communication is as simple as picking up a phone or newspaper, or hooking into a modem. There is a continual turnover of homes for sale, and buyers for them.

The real-estate agent is no longer necessary. Old ideas die hard, however. Many of us also grew up believing that mothers should stay at home and raise the children. A nice idea, but no longer financially feasible for the average family.

No one said that selling a home is simple. Neither is repairing one's car or television set. However, before you decide to list with a real-estate agency, you should give careful consideration to your reasons. Force of habit can be very costly.

Selling your own home requires commitment and patience. You must be prepared to take on the tasks that a real-estate agent would perform. These tasks are not complicated, but do take time. However, the rewards of doing it yourself are great. We are talking about a saving of literally thousands of tax-free dollars.

LACK OF INFORMATION

I'm convinced that, if more people knew how to go about it, they would sell their own homes. No one should undertake such a major project without guidelines. Information regarding how to sell your own home has been scarce until the present time. This book will help to get you organized, and on your way.

FEAR OF UNDERPRICING

Some homeowners are afraid of underpricing their homes. They nurture a feeling of security and trust in the traditional real-estate institution. Often, this is a false sense of security, based on lack of knowledge. There are no guarantees that someone else can get a better price for your home than you can. In fact, if you take the real-estate commission into account, it is impossible for you to get top dollar for your home, because, no matter what the final selling price is, you must still subtract 6% or 7% from the profit. Wouldn't you like to sell your home for the same price, and keep the commission for yourself?

You can. Establishing a fair price for your home is simple (refer to Chapter 4 for details). You certainly don't need to hire a real-estate agent to do this for you.

LACK OF INCENTIVE

If you're fortunate enough to have someone else footing the bill for the cost of selling your home, you probably have no interest in taking on the job yourself. This is understandable. However, it may be worth your while to check the terms of the selling arrangements. For example, if your company has had your home appraised for $142,000 and you think you can get $149,000 on your own, some companies will allow you to keep the difference. Look into the possibilities before you brush off the idea of selling your own home.

FEAR OF LEGAL PAPERWORK

Some people are intimidated by the legal aspects of selling a house. All the legal language and real-estate laws seem too complex, and present an insurmountable obstacle to selling on your own. This fear is based on lack of knowledge.

Even if you hire a real-estate agent to sell your home, you will still require a lawyer's assistance in completing legal documents on your behalf. Before you pass on the idea of selling your home, give your lawyer a call. Explain that you want to sell your own home, and ask if he or she can be of help to you. You might be pleasantly surprised to find that many lawyers are very willing to give you all the help you will need, for a fraction of the real-estate commission.

LACK OF TIME

If you don't have the time to answer phone calls and show your house yourself, find a good real-estate agent. Selling a home *does* require commitment. If you go through the bother of placing an advertisement in the newspaper and you can't be home to handle inquiries, you're wasting your time and money.

To be successful, you must put a potential buyer's concerns ahead of yours. This might mean showing the home at a time when you would rather be doing something else. If you're not prepared to devote at least some of your evenings to selling, over a four to eight week period, then don't even start.

There is a place for real-estate agencies. If you simply do not have the time or interest in doing it on your own, hire a professional to do it for you. Or, if you open your mouth only long enough to put your other foot in, it may be wise to let someone else take over. If, for whatever reason, your home is difficult to sell, let an experienced person take on the headache. In any case, using a real-estate agent should be considered a luxury, not a necessity.

CHAPTER 2

THE REAL ESTATE GAME

Why do you need a real-estate agent? Let's take a closer look at the services provided by the average real-estate company:

ADVERTISING AND PROMOTION

Once you've agreed to list your home, the real-estate agent will compose a brief summary of your home, and advertise it. This includes advertising in the local newspaper and in the real-estate office. Many agents will suggest an "open house," in which time is allocated to allow the public access to your home for a few hours, without prior appointment. It also includes the lawn sign, which generally does more to promote the particular real-estate company than your home. However, it does give you the impression that the real-estate agent is doing something to earn the money.

There's nothing complicated about advertising. With some thought, you can come up with a brief description of your home, and put your ad in the newspapers and many free places, such as community centres, grocery stores, public billboards and so on.

Accurately describing your home is not a difficult task, merely one which requires some practice and attention to detail.

SHOWING THE HOME TO POTENTIAL BUYERS

The real-estate agent takes potential buyers on a tour through your home, for the purpose of selling. Showing your home is not difficult (see Chapter 8). It requires preparation and some finesse, but that's all. Although the first time is likely to be nerve-racking, it does get easier with each visitor.

Real-estate agents will offer suggestions in advance as to how to make your home "show well." Often, they will give you a standard brochure on painting, cleaning up, and other tips to help improve the appeal of your home. That should suggest that preparing a home for the purpose of selling is not mysterious, but simply requires common sense, combined with an awareness of how a potential buyer would view your home. You don't have to pay 6% of the total selling price of your home to acquire this knowledge.

Ultimately, you do necessary repairs yourself, or pay to have someone else prepare the house. I have yet to see the real-estate agent who offers to pick up a paintbrush to help you get the house ready. That isn't her job. Agents will *advise*, but won't get their hands dirty. Very expensive advice, that you can obtain on your own.

ESTABLISHING A SELLING PRICE

The real-estate agent will suggest a selling price for your home. Most will base the price upon the market analysis. That is, a price based upon comparable houses that have been sold in a similar neighbourhood. Unlike you, the agent must consider the amount of effort required to sell the home. Obviously, the lower the asking price, the quicker the sale. It's in the real-estate agent's best interest to get you to lower your asking price. It makes the job easier.

Real-estate agents are caught in the middle between seller and buyer. Naturally, the seller wants the highest price possible for his home, while the buyer is looking for a bargain. The agent has to convince potential buyers that your house is worth more than they want to pay for it. Which is easier? Wearing out your tongue trying to sell an expensive house to an uncommitted stranger, or preparing yourself in advance by talking down the pricc of the house before putting it on the market?

This is done as part of the market analysis. The agent tries to cut through your emotional attachment to your house and convince you to see it realistically. This is reasonable. However, some unscrupulous agents may counter your home's strong points (which you think will escalate the price) by saying that nicer homes than yours have been sold for less money. For every reason you give to justify a higher price for your home, the agent will counter with one which supports his or her lower estimate.

Although it all seems very scientific and highly sophisticated, such an assessment may be far from accurate. A real-estate agent is *not* a professional appraiser. A market analysis is not a formal appraisal (see Chapter 4 for details).

Consider my experience with the first real-estate agent who did a market analysis on my home. My pride and joy was my jacuzzi room. She examined it and said, "You must have at least $5,000 in this room." I was impressed by her accuracy. She then added, "Too bad it's in such a small house." She was belittling what I considered my best selling feature.

Feeling very numbed by this experience, I obtained two other market analyses from separate realty companies. Of the three, the first was the lowest estimate (to the tune of 12%). She called me back to ask if I wanted to sell with her. I told her that her estimate was far too low to seriously consider. Perhaps her negative comment about my jacuzzi room was a tactic to get me to lower my asking price. However, I interpreted it quite differently. If she was already minimizing my home's most outstanding feature, how could she show the rest of the house with confidence? I knew my bungalow was not a palace, but so what? In retrospect, I will admit that the attitude of that real-estate agent was the biggest impetus toward my decision to sell my own house. After all, I couldn't do any worse.

To further persuade you that a market-analysis price is not etched in stone, invite a few opinions from different real-estate companies. Since these market analyses are provided free of charge, you have nothing to lose. Even if you decide to sell with a real-estate agent, it's in your best interest to get a minimum of three estimates. An informed homeowner is in a better bargaining position when it comes to settling on asking price.

You can establish your own price, confidently and accurately. If, despite all efforts, you aren't sure what to ask, your best bet is to get a formal appraisal. This is an impartial assessment of your home by an *expert*. Although this will cost \$150 to \$200, you are paying for a valuable, reliable service, which will give you the peace of mind you seek. On the other hand, blindly accepting the first market-analysis estimate as the price for which you will sell your home, may cost you thousands of dollars in the long run.

Thus, you don't need to hire a real-estate agent to help you set a price for your home.

ARRANGE FINANCING

The real-estate agent will take on the headache of screening buyers and arranging financing, once a buyer has been found.

This service is completely unnecessary. Many agents claim that they have already screened potential buyers before they have a look at your home; that is, they have checked into the buyer's financial status and income, and determined that this person can afford to buy your home. This is not always the case. Hiring a real-estate agent provides no guarantees that you will find the perfect buyer (unless the buyer is well known to the agent). It's very difficult to accurately assess whether or not someone can afford your home. Someone who appears to earn a good income may be up to his ears in debt. A potential buyer is under no obligation to divulge such personal information to a real-estate agent.

Ultimately, once an offer has been made on your home, if the buyer wishes to take out a mortgage, it is the mortgagee (bank or mortgage company) who determines whether or not the buyer can afford your home. You don't need a real-estate agent for any part of this process.

Even if you hire an agent, you'll still require a lawyer's help in completing the necessary legal documents. It's much cheaper to ask your lawyer for any help you might need than to turn to a real-estate agent.

To summarize;

Using a real-estate agent should be considered a luxury, not a necessity, because:

a. you can do your own advertising,
b. you can prepare your own home for show, and show it yourself,
c. you can figure out what you want for an asking price,
d. hiring a real-estate agent provides no guarantee that you will find a perfect buyer, who can afford your home, and
e. even if you use a real-estate agent, you will still need a lawyer's help in completing legal documents related to the sale of the house. If you hire a lawyer exclusively, you'll save yourself a small fortune.

PSYCHOLOGICAL ROADBLOCKS

Understandably, most people are nervous about the idea of selling their homes. Besides the fear of the unknown, thousands of dollars are at stake, and there is the real fear of making a bad deal.

Typical comments. . .
"I'd feel too ill at ease showing my own house."
"I don't know what price to ask."
"I don't know how to barter, and would probably get snowed by a sharp talker."
"I don't understand real estate or legal language."
"The whole idea is too intimidating. After all, if it's easy, why doesn't everyone sell their own home?"

Some real-estate agents play on these fears, and may discourage you before you've even had a chance to try. Sometime during the selling of your house you may have to interact with real-estate agents. I'd like to point out some scenarios you may face, and create another point of view that will give you something to fight back with.

Most real-estate agents who would like to sell your house don't give up easily. No one can blame them, either. They're simply trying to earn a living. Since there is not a real need for their service, they must create a need, by making you feel incompetent to take on the job. I've explained the tasks they do on your behalf and pointed out that you can do them yourself.

Argument #1

> "We are experts at selling homes. You are not. Selling a home is more difficult than you think."

So what if you are not an expert? There's no law that states you have to be an expert to sell your own home. After all, you're only selling one house—yours—which you have lived in and with for years. Who better knows its foibles and strong points than you, who has spent season after season;

trimming the hedges,
cutting the lawn,
shovelling sidewalks,
lounging in the bathtub,
storing items in the lazy Susans,
cleaning the windows,
admiring the view,
paying hydro and gas bills,
planting flowers,
sitting by the fireplace,
paying the mortgage,
making barbeques in the backyard,
folding clothes in the laundry room,
installing speakers in the rec room,

entertaining in the living room,
refinishing the basement,
fixing the toilet?

You have—not the "expert." You are not taking on the job of selling strange homes, belonging to strangers, in strange neighbourhoods, to other strangers. You don't have to be a smooth talker. *The house will sell itself,* on its own merits. All you have to do is dress it up, show it off, and know your price. You need to be sincere, not glib—to have good business sense, not fanfare. You're selling a valuable, marketable product—your home—not some fly-by-night unnecessary piece of junk. You need direction and advice, not a degree or a diploma.

Do you have to be a gourmet chef to prepare an attractive meal? For this, you have cookbooks (the original do-it-yourself manual). Do you have to be a certified mechanic to change a tire on your car? Of course not. However, if you were changing someone else's tire and wanted to charge for your service, you would need some kind of proof as to your qualifications. *You don't need a licence to sell your own home*. The expert does.

I'll tell you how I sold my own home. I don't know if I could sell a strange house. To me, it would involve a great deal of work—work in which I am not interested. When it's your house, you care deeply, and the main ingredients are *caring, confidence and good direction.* The caring you have already, the confidence you will acquire with experience, and as to direction—I'll light the candle and point the way.

Argument #2

"XYZ Realty has sold thousands of homes. . . ."

The real-estate market has become extremely competitive. Real-estate companies try not only to persuade you not to sell your own home, but also to talk you into letting them, rather than the competition, sell it for you.

Consider the content of most real-estate advertisements;

WE ARE FRIENDLY
WE ARE EXPERTS
WE UNDERSTAND YOUR FAMILY AND THEIR NEEDS
WE ARE REPUTABLE
XYZ REALTY HAS SOLD MANY HOMES
LET US SELL YOURS

The message? We will sell your home by using our institutional reputation. *Brand name* selling. Let's take a closer look.

Institutional prestige, or name dropping, is often used by real-estate agents to persuade you to sell with their company (and thus with them). In this society, we are inundated with all varieties of brand name advertising. With brand name buying comes a bigger price tag. The counter to this is the emergence of the generic or "no–name" brand. You don't pay for the expensive promotion and packaging of the product, and therefore it costs less. What this country needs is a good No–Name Real-Estate Company.

Think about what you get if you decide to list your home with XYZ Realty. An individual agent is selling your home—not XYZ Realty. Although the agent may be a representative of the most successful real-estate company in the country, there's no guarantee that the individual who is selling your home is a top-notch salesman.

There's no law against screening real-estate agents. Ask them how long they have been in the business; how many homes they've sold, and for what price; how long it took; what was the original asking price of the home. Then check up on it. Make a decision whether or not to use a real-estate agent based on individual merits—not merely the institutional brand name. Don't be blinded by slick advertising. You may be pleasantly surprised to find that you aren't so different from the agent.

Argument #3

"We have a corner on the market."

"People who want to buy a home come to us first. We have 85% of the buyers already waiting. If you advertise, you'll get, at most 15% of the buyers".

This is true. Real-estate companies do have access to more buyers than you do. However, you need only one person to buy your house. A larger population is no guarantee that the right buyer is waiting to buy your home. And it isn't worth 6% of the total value of your home to find out.

Argument #4

"You might get a lot of lookers, but you won't get serious offers."

Real-estate agents will use third-party intervention as a tactic to justify selling your home. How does this work?

Impartial Third Party: Real-estate agents will argue that serious buyers will not want to insult the homeowner by criticizing features of your home in front of you. Buyers feel uneasy making an offer, because they don't want to deal with owner wrath, if the offer is too low.

"That's where we come in. We show your home, and take the client back to the car. We ask them what they think and they tell us the truth—that they like your house, but they don't like the kitchen cupboards—and we ask them to make an offer."

It may be true that some potential buyers will feel ill at ease criticizing something as personal as your home, but this depends on your attitude when you show it. If your house doesn't suit the needs of the buyers, they won't put in an offer, either to you or to the real-estate agent. Through no fault of your own or of the house, it simply isn't what they need, and no amount of talking will convince them otherwise.

Buyers should not be forced or pressured into buying your home. They'll regret it later. If the buyer is not interested in your home, back off. Thank him or her for coming over to see the house and don't waste any more time.

On the other hand, perhaps a buyer likes everything in your house, except the kitchen cupboards. This can be a negotiating feature (drop the price by what it costs to replace the cupboards) if you do want to sell it to them.

Comparison: This is another technique based on third-party intervention. If a buyer is interested in your house, but is undecided, the real-estate agent will argue that he or she can show the buyer other similar homes, and demonstrate that your house is the best buy. The buyer will then have other homes with which to compare yours. What do you do if you're trying to sell your own home in this case? How can you compete with this service?

This is a valid point. I can't think of anyone who has two similar homes for sale at the same time. However, I gave my buyers more credit than the real-estate agent did. Many people who came by "for a look" had already seen many homes. They made their own comparisons. Or they saw my home, went off on their own and looked at several others, and then came back again. *The house will sell itself, based on its own merits, and on the price.* These were informed buyers. It gave them more negotiating power to say, "I really like this house. I saw another house similar to yours at 64 Main Street, but it didn't have a finished basement. However, they were asking $5,000 less." This is a serious buyer, who is sending you buying signals. You don't need a real-estate agent to tell you this.

The selling–by–comparison technique can work against you. Don't forget, the real-estate agent makes his living selling homes, and is trying to sell more than one house at a time. When the agent brings a buyer over for a look, how can you be sure that your house isn't the example being shown to sell someone else's house? The real-estate agent may play double jeopardy—making you believe that he is trying to sell your home by bringing serious buyers over to look, when the buyers are more interested in someone else's house. You're being used, and you don't even know it.

It sounds callous, but it's reality. It's important to understand, because you must appreciate the position of the person selling your home. Unlike you, the agent must continually generate business to stay in business. After a customer has looked over your home, and gone back in the real-estate agent's car to discuss your house, the conversation might go like this;

Agent: Well, what do you think?

Client: It's a nice house, but I don't know. They're asking for a lot of money.

Agent: What would you be prepared to offer?

Client: I don't know. I think I'm changing my mind. Maybe a smaller house with a built-in dishwasher would be more what we need.

Agent: I've got another house that's just what you're looking for. Let's go have a quick look.

To stay alive in business, the real-estate agent has to think of himself. He says he's working for you. This is true. He's also working for himself. The agent must make the buyer think he is getting a good deal. Otherwise, the buyer may end up regretting his decision, and blame the agent for giving him a raw deal. Word of mouth is an important form of advertising in the real-state industry. Sooner or later, this particular buyer will want to sell, or will have friends who want to sell their home. Do you think he's going to hire (or recommend) a real-estate agent who didn't act (or appear to act) in his best interest? The real-estate agent is playing a very complicated game, necessary to his business survival.

For you, it's a much simpler matter. You don't have to worry about generating future business, or conducting concurrent business. For you, there is no conflict of interest. You have only one thing to concentrate on: the sale of your home. Potential buyers know this. You can afford to be honest and direct. Playing games isn't necessary.

Argument #5

"Buyers don't like to deal directly with the owner."

Think about this. When you were shopping around to buy your first home, where were the owners? Were they out of the house? Were they somewhere in the background, watching TV or reading the paper? If they were in the house, didn't you feel just a little bit ill at ease while you were going through the home? Didn't you feel like you were invading their privacy? Weren't you relieved when it came time to leave? Why did you feel this way? Wouldn't you have felt better if you had talked to the owners, or had them show you their home?

As the homeowner, the real-estate agent wants you to believe that you make potential buyers feel uncomfortable. As the vendor, you're the bad guy. The agent is the good guy—the fair, impartial voice of reason.

Baloney. By his very presence in your home, the agent is creating an artificial situation. Years ago, the real-estate agent filled a need by bringing together buyer and seller. This was a time during which homes for sale were scarce, and methods of communication were limited.

Far from bringing together the buyer and seller, the agent now creates an atmosphere of unnecessary distrust between them. Unless direct negotiation is impossible, because of emotionally laden circumstances (e.g., marital separations, child custody cases), talking face to face is always the best way to do business—not through a third party.

You are selling a home. Someone else wants to buy a home. Why do you need someone to talk on your behalf?

Argument #6

"We have experience selling homes. You don't."

This depends on the level of experience of the individual real-estate agent. Even if the agent has been selling homes for twenty years, remember, you aren't giving up your job to go into the real-estate business. You're selling one home—yours. At one time, even the most experienced real-estate agent was selling his first house. How does that differ from what you're trying to accomplish?

You have an advantage the real-estate agent lacks. It's your house. *You may not have experience in selling homes, but you have experience in living in and with your product.*

Argument #7

> "We know how to show your house effectively. No one can be objective when they are selling their own home. Why, even I hire a real-estate agent to sell my house."

No special training is required to show a home, or any product. The principles involved in showing and selling do not depend on the product. Regardless of whether you are selling encyclopaedias or a house, the principles are the same. These include;

a. knowing the product well,
b. knowing what the product is worth,
c. having confidence in the product,
d. conveying an interest in the product, and
e. creating a need for the product.

The ability to sound professional comes from knowing the facts about your house. Even if you were selling a bicycle, if you couldn't provide pertinent facts, such as age and tire size, you would make a poor impression on potential buyers, and they would look elsewhere.

Now, more specifically, the sale of your home. Consider the statement: "We know how to show your property." What, exactly, do real-estate agents know about your property? How did they acquire this knowledge? They will go to the local city hall or the registry office, and obtain easily accessible documents (available to the public) regarding the particulars of your house; the type of construction, age, style, amperage, property taxes, and so on. The bare bones of the house.

Any other information the real-estate agent has about your house, he has because you have supplied it. However, you've lived in the home. You are an *expert* in living in the home and neighbourhood. No home is an island. Buyers ask questions about the neighbours; location of the nearest convenience stores, if the post office is within walking distance, are the streets cleaned during the winter, and so forth. You will be able to answer such questions with ease. You aren't a stranger, the real-estate agent is.

Argument #8

"We will get a better price for your home, than if you sell on your own."

If you are realistic about the price you want for your house, this is not true. Think about it. You want $187,000 for your home. If you have to pay an additional 6% for the cost of the commission, you must add an additional $11,220 to $187,000 to realize the same profit.

What if the mortgagee (buyer's bank or mortgage company) appraises your home at $187,000? You'll find it very difficult to justify selling your home for 6% more than its appraised value, unless the buyer is prepared to pay cash or give a 25% down payment (see Chapter 14—Why Deals Fall Through).

Many buyers opt to make a 10% down payment on a house, and look for mortgage financing to pay the difference. Most banks will extend mortgage financing based upon the appraised value of the home (90% of $187,000). If you are asking $198,220 (to cover the realtor's fee), the buyer will have to come up with cash to pay the difference between your sale price and the bank's appraised price.

It's important to keep in mind that most Offers to Purchase are conditional upon the buyer's ability to obtain financing, and the sale price of the house *not exceeding* the price set by the independent appraisal (required by the mortgagee prior to granting mortgage approval).

In other words, if you house is worth $187,000 according to the appraised value, and you are selling the home for $198,220, *the buyer can legally back out of the deal.* Or, the buyer might still want to buy your house at its assessed value—$187,000, not $198,220. This is fair. So you end up selling your home for $187,000 and still have to pay $11,220 for the commission.

Unless you are selling the house for *less* than it's worth, the real-estate agent will *not* get a better price. It's impossible. There are clauses that protect buyers from purchasing grossly overpriced homes, unless they wish to pay cash for the house.

> The best the real estate agent can do is sell your house for what it's worth, *minus* the commission fee.

Deciding what price to put on your home is not a mystery. Real-estate agents use the same methods described in Chapter 4. Real-estate agents know it's unethical, if not impossible, to sell a home for more than its appraised value.

Although I have yet to meet the real-estate agent who would admit it, the best he or she can do for you is to sell the house for the top appraised value, less the commission.

> Unless you sell your home for less than its appraised value, you will not make more money by hiring a real-estate agent. You will make less.

Argument #9

> "We prevent unscrupulous buyers from taking advantage of you."
>
> "Some buyers comb through the classifieds, looking for a private sale. They know you don't have to pay a commission, and will use this information against you to get you to lower your price."

Everyone's looking for a bargain. Why not? Far from being a disadvantage, selling your home on your own will probably be one of your biggest drawing cards—and one that the real-estate agent cannot provide. Why shouldn't a potential buyer be attracted to a home that may be thousands of dollars cheaper, because realty fees are not involved?

Know your asking price and your rock-bottom price. Allow room to negotiate. Don't be greedy. "But I did all the work just to save the commission, not to split it with someone else." If you are adamant about not sharing part of your savings, be prepared to spend significantly more time selling your home. You want to get a fair price for the house. So does the buyer. A successful business deal enables both parties to benefit. No one feels taken. Don't try to get rich overnight from the sale of one house.

A house is probably the biggest investment you have

ever made. If you're like most people, you will own only a few homes in your lifetime. Selling your home on your own can be one of the most financially rewarding experiences of your life.

As long as your house is in demand and structurally sound, and market conditions are healthy (annual increases of 7% or better on the price of homes, mortgage financing interest rates not beyond reach), your house will increase in value as a function of time alone.

You are the one who has paid interest on the mortgage all these years. *You* are the one who has put time and money into maintaining the house. Simply by living in and caring for the home, you have already done half of the work of selling. Why short-change yourself by hiring a real-estate agent?

There is a place for real-estate services. If you're in a terrible rush, and cannot devote time to preparing and showing the house—get thee to a real-estate agency. Or, if you think you'll get rich by selling your own home, let the real-estate people help you. You'll save months of time, but you still won't get rich.

But, if time is not a factor, you can sell your house on your own. Especially if you have an average income, the thousands of tax-free dollars you'll save by selling it yourself will represent weeks or months of savings.

Some people will drive miles out of their way to save thirty cents on a jar of coffee, but miss out on legal income-tax deductions worth hundreds of dollars, because they don't take the time to read and understand. Many have a mental block to taking on new projects that will greatly increase their sense of confidence and well-being, as well as their bank balances.

Give up your conditioned beliefs. If you are willing to learn, you don't need to hire someone to fix your toaster. You don't need to hire someone to sell your home either. A real-estate agency is a luxury, not a necessity. It's an emergency measure, if you don't have time. If you try selling your home and give up, it's always a backup measure. You can always resort to a realtor. There's lots of competition, hungry for another listing.

Selling your own house will take time. But for most, it's a good investment. There are very few experiences that match the exhilaration and sense of personal pride of selling your own home. And then, there's the money. . . .

Chapter Summary

1. Using a real-estate agent should be considered a luxury, not a necessity.

2. You don't need to be an expert to sell your own home.

3. You don't require a licence to sell your own home. The real-estate agent does.

4. The principles involved in selling a house are the same as selling anything else.

5. You know more about your home than you think you do. Don't underestimate this knowledge when it comes time to sell.

6. Any legal matters that arise during the process of selling can easily be dealt with by your lawyer. Even if you use a real-estate agent, ultimately, you will also require a lawyer's assistance to complete the legal documents. If you use a lawyer exclusively, you'll save yourself a great deal of money.

7. The mortgagee (bank or mortgage company) will arrange financing for the buyer. Financing is the buyer's responsibility, for which real-estate services are not required.

8. There is no guarantee that a real-estate agent can screen the "perfect buyer" for you.

9. A real-estate agent is not a professional appraiser. Therefore, the price quoted for your home, based on a market analysis, may not be accurate. Get at least three separate opinions before making up your mind.

10. There's no reason to assume that a real-estate agent can get a better price for your house than you can. The best the real-estate agent can do is sell your house for what it's worth, minus the 6% commission.

CHAPTER 3

GETTING IN TOUCH WITH YOUR HOME

You've made the decision. You're going to sell the house on your own. Exactly what do you have to offer? You've probably owned your home for a few years. After a while, you start taking the nice things for granted, and turning a blind eye to some of the less desirable aspects of your home. In other words, you've learned to live in and with your house as it is.

To sell successfully, it's essential that you see your house as others will see it. First of all, you must regard your home as a house. That is, you must be able to look at it as a marketable product, in competition with others.

How do you begin to see your home objectively? I recommend Russell Oddy's (*For Sale by Owner*) idea of taking a notebook in hand and going on a sight-seeing tour through your house, jotting down all of the desirable and undesirable features of each room. Repeat this process for both the front yard and back yard.

You now have a starting point: a tangible list of the advantages and disadvantages of your house and property. This may be the first time you've noticed that loose handrail, or how the front door could stand a fresh coat of paint. Alternatively, you may have overlooked the beautiful mantle above your fireplace.

BACK TO BASICS

In addition to appearance, you must familiarize yourself with the structure of the house. Buyers are certain to inquire about the age of the home, insulation, amperage, type and age of plumbing, condition of furnace and water heater, and so on. This information can easily be acquired through your local city hall, or registry office, where such records are stored. You will obtain a detailed sheet of facts about your house, which includes all of the above, plus other useful information.

Buyers frequently ask about the cost of heating the home. I would suggest collecting your heat, water and utilities bills for the past year. In this way, the buyer gets a realistic idea of how much it costs to heat the home during the year's coldest months. It also makes you look well organized.

FINANCES

Gather together all your legal documents about the house, such as the mortgage papers, surveyor's certificate, and the like. If you can't find them, make an appointment to talk with your lawyer or bank manager, who will provide you with copies. If you have a mortgage, review the conditions and clauses. For example, with a closed mortgage, you may have to pay a "pay-out" penalty, if you sell your home before the mortgage is renewable. If you aren't sure where you stand, check with your bank manager.

Buyers are usually very interested in knowing the amount of your property taxes. Be prepared. Knowing the financial facts behind your home reassures buyers that you know what you're doing.

Your goal is to get to know your house, inside and out. There are two important reasons for this: to see your home realistically, so you can sell it for a fair price; and to be well-informed, in order to present your home professionally and confidently when it comes time to show.

CHAPTER 4

SETTING A PRICE

How do you decide what your home is worth in dollars and cents? You might be emotionally, as well as financially, invested in your home. To arrive at a fair selling price, it's necessary to rely strictly upon financial, rather than emotional, parameters.

The two most important figure to establish are:

a. the highest amount you could reasonably expect to get for the house; and
b. the lowest amount you would accept for the house—your "rock-bottom" price.

The first figure should be your asking price. This is the amount you quote in your ads, and to interested parties. When the time comes for serious bartering over the price, the second figure is your bottom line. *Do not divulge your bottom price to anyone*. This figure is only to be used as an aid to your mental preparation. From the outset, many buyers will 'test the water," so to speak, and will try to determine how cheaply you will sell the house, before they make an offer. If you state your rock-bottom price, that's exactly what you'll end up with.

Prior to selling your home, decide how low you can afford to go, so that, when you discuss price, you won't have to waste valuable time deciding whether or not to seriously consider or accept an offer. Alternatively, if you haven't determined your rock-bottom price ahead of time, you will find negotiating the final price to be a nerve-wracking and frustrating experience, which will be shared equally by the potential buyer (see Chapter 11 for additional information).

To help you determine price, consider the real estate commission (6% on average). You can afford to be flexible in both asking and rock-bottom price, since you're saving the 6% realty fee. If you want to sell the home very quickly, you can sell it for slightly less than its actual appraised worth, and still earn money, because of this. You won't realize as large a profit, but you won't lose. Keep this plan as a back-up option. If you can afford to spend four to eight weeks of your time, list your house at its appraised value. You can always drop the price later, if absolutely necessary.

Consider the following equation:

ORIGINAL PURCHASE PRICE	+	COST OF HOME IMPROVEMENTS	=	MINIMUM SELLING PRICE
$70,000		$7,000		$77,000

An oversimplified way of determining your home's worth is to add the amount you originally paid for the house, plus any home improvement costs incurred since the original purchase. This total will enable you to break even on the sale of your house. However, this assumes that your original purchase price was fair—that you neither overpaid nor underpaid for the house.

This equation does not take into account how many years you've owned the house, or the current market value. Since most homes increase in value, as a function of time alone, if you bought your home twelve years ago, it would be absurd to sell it merely for the original asking price, plus improvements.

A more reasonable equation would be the following;

CURRENT APPRAISED VALUE & MARKET CONDITIONS	+	SUPPLY & DEMAND	=	MAXIMUM ASKING PRICE

This equation takes into account the present value of your house, compared to similar homes. It takes into account consumer demand and supply. Obviously, if many people want to buy, the houses are in low supply, the house is worth more.

Regardless of what you originally paid for the house, you will have to stick by these parameters. For example, if the economy was booming in your town when you bought your home, but is now a victim of recession, you cannot expect to make the profit you may have anticipated. You must be realistic in setting your price. If you're greedy, and ask for an amount well above what anyone else would consider a fair price, you will find yourself alone at the bargaining table.

MARKET ANALYSIS

If you still don't have a price in mind, don't panic. A good method of determining price is to invite different real-estate companies to provide you with a market analysis. Since the real-estate business is highly competitive, most realtors offer this service free of charge, in order to help you make up your mind to sell with their company. This is what happens. The real-estate agent comes to your home, walks through all the rooms and the front and back yard. Some may bring tape measures, and actually measure each room in the house. The entire process takes approximately fifteen minutes. The agent will get in touch with you a day or so later, after getting all the particulars (age of house, actual lot size, etc.). You will then be given an estimate of what the agent feels the house is worth, usually within a range of a few thousand dollars, plus a brief description of your home, with suggestions for home improvements. Please keep in mind that this is an *opinion*. It's very important to obtain at least three market analyses from separate realtors. In this way, you will have a basis for comparison. If all three quotes are similar, you have more assurance that the asking price is realistic. If there is a marked variation in opinion (more than three or four thousand dollars), question the agent as to why the estimate is so much higher or lower. It doesn't hurt to understand an agent's rationalization of the price he or she has set. At this point, you have not committed yourself to selling with any realtor, so you have nothing to lose.

Be leery of the agent who promises an extraordinarily high price for your home. It may be that the agent simply wishes to get your house listed with the realtor, and is not realistic about the asking price. The house will never sell at a price that's not in keeping with similar homes.

As mentioned earlier, even if you opt to have a real-estate company sell your house, it's in your best interest to get three separate market analyses. A knowledgeable home-owner will not be intimidated by real-estate agents, and is in a far better position to get the best deal possible for the house.

FORMAL APPRAISAL

An appraisal is not the same as a market analysis. It's an independent assessment of your home by a professionally trained and licensed individual who does not represent a real-estate company. In addition to evaluating fixed aspects of the home (lot size, house size, location, etc.), the appraiser will inspect your home, measures all the rooms, and take into consideration special features, such as a fireplace or new renovations. He or she will arrive at what is considered the fairest price for the house, given current market conditions.

The appraiser has nothing to gain by underpricing or overpricing your home. Unlike a real-estate agent, there is no conflict of interest involved in setting the current price of your home. Formal appraisals are used by banks and other mortgaging companies to determine a house's actual worth, prior to mortgage approval.

Although this method is not infallible, acquiring a formal appraisal is certainly your best means of determining what price to ask for your house. The only disadvantage is the cost—approximately $150 to $200, at the time of this writing. This may seem expensive but, in the long run, you may save thousands of dollars. At least you will be buying the best unbiased opinion possible. I shudder to think of the thousands of dollars I would have lost, had I taken my first market analysis opinion to heart, and sold the house for that amount.

A second reason for obtaining a formal appraisal is to provide a written assurance for buyers. Some buyers are quite leery of private sales. They worry that the home is overpriced. You can reassure potential buyers that you are asking a fair price for the home, by showing them a copy of the formal appraised value. This also gives you more credibility as a vendor.

One final consideration. Unless a buyer is prepared to pay cash for your house or 25% of the total value as the down payment, a formal appraisal is required by the bank or mortgage company, prior to granting mortgage approval. If your asking price is significantly above the appraised value, most offers of purchase contain a clause that permits the buyer to legally back out of the deal. Although the intent is to protect the mortgagee from making a poor investment, it also protects the buyer from making a bad deal. A practical consideration is that most banks will only provide 90% of the purchase price, based on the appraised value. If you're asking $5000 above the appraised value, buyers have to come up with this additional cash out of their pockets (if they still want to buy your house, since they are no longer legally bound to honour the purchase of sale contract).

If you've overpriced your house, you'll find yourself in the embarrassing position of having to justify the high price. Paying for a formal appraisal gives you the assurance that you are asking a fair price.

ALTERNATIVES

Not everyone has to get a formal appraisal or market analysis to come up with a realistic price tag for his or her house. You can do it yourself if you're willing to do a lot of leg-work. Check the newspapers for homes similar to yours that are for sale. See what price they're asking. Better yet, visit the homes that are offering an open house. You'll get a first hand look at what X dollars will buy.

Go to different real-estate companies, and look at the listings and descriptions. In addition to homes currently for sale, most real-estate companies display ads for homes they have sold. Most will state the asking price and the eventual selling price. This gives you a good idea of the amount you can expect to get for your home.

Chapter Summary

1. The two most important figures to determine are your asking price and rock-bottom price.

2. Never reveal your rock-bottom price. This is only to be used as your personal guideline for negotiating a final price.

3. If you're in a rush to sell, you can always decrease the asking price by a portion of the 6% commission. You won't make as large a profit, but you certainly won't lose money.

4. Take advantage of free market analyses provided by most real-estate companies. Even if you decide to sell with a realtor, you will be better informed if you acquire a minimum of three opinions.

5. Although a formal appraisal will cost money, it's your best guarantee for an unbiased, accurate assessment of your home's actual worth on the current market.

6. Unless you have a buyer willing to pay cash, or put a 25% down-payment on your home, a formal appraisal will be required by the mortgagee, prior to granting mortgage approval. It is unethical and extremely difficult to sell your home for an amount exceeding its actual worth. Don't be greedy. Be fair.

CHAPTER 5

PREPARING THE PRODUCT

How are you going to market your product for sale? If you are in a great rush, you might forego giving your home a face-lift and sell it as a handyman special. If you wish to get the best price for your house, you must put in the extra effort. Be prepared to undertake whatever repair jobs are necessary; paint, polish, clean, clean, and more clean.

WHY A FACELIFT IS NECESSARY

"First impressions are important," is a common expression. Nothing could be more true when it comes to selling a home. Consider two used cars for sale. They are identical, except that one has an immaculate interior and a hard wax finish, with chrome that gleams. Which of the two will sell more quickly, and for a better price? The answer is obvious.

You're selling the house on your own. You can afford to put to good use a few of the thousands of dollars you would have paid as a real-estate commission. Investing a small sum in sensible home improvement projects will help to sell your home quickly, and often for a modestly higher price.

Dramatically improving the look of your house does not need to be expensive. It's amazing how a few gallons of paint can give a fresh, bright look to a house. Minor repairs to dripping faucets, and regrouting tubs, leave a buyer less concerned about the overall adequacy of the plumbing. Clearing out all the useless junk in the backyard can magically make it look larger and more appealing.

It's easy to rationalize putting off minor repairs and improvements. You may feel that all your work will be for nothing, since the new owners will probably change the home to suit their tastes. This is *not* true. If you want top dollar for your house, expect to put in the effort to make it worth the asking price.

IDENTIFYING NEEDS FOR HOME IMPROVEMENT

If you have lived in your home for a few years, you have probably developed a comfortable sort of relationship with it, and have learned to ignore minor irritations like that squeak in the floorboard.

To attain the objectivity necessary to see what needs to be done, to ensure your home will look its best, it's essential to see your house as others see it.

How do you learn to see your house like a potential buyer? How does a home—your home—revert to being just another house?

I hope that you've taken a tour through your home and yard, and compiled a list of all the attributes and drawbacks. If not, please do so now. If you do not find this exercise useful, it's time to do some field work. Check the newspaper ads for open houses that are similar to yours. Go and have a look for yourself. It may be easier to identify your own home's strengths and weaknesses after you've compared what you have to offer with other homes already on the market.

A third suggestion, if you have not already done so, is to take advantage of a few free market analyses. As part of these analyses, real-estate agents provide you with a list of home improvement suggestions. They usually give you a brochure containing standard ideas on home improvement. Often these are *very* useful. You will also get a few opinions as to whether or not you need to do major repairs, such as retiling the bathroom.

Get organized. Write a list of improvements that you plan to undertake. If you plan to do more than paint and clean, obtain a few cost estimates for materials and labour, in order to establish a total cost of the repairs.

BEST-RETURN PROJECTS

Before you run to the bank for a home improvement loan, it's wise to consider what type of projects will give you the best return on your money. Your kitchen cupboards may not win a place in *Better Homes & Gardens*, but if you cannot hope to recover improvement costs in the eventual selling price of the house, there's no reason for undertaking such major renovations. Be content with less involved, but more cost-effective, improvements.

However, if your house has serious maintenance problems, such as plumbing or wiring defects, these must be repaired, or the buyer notified in advance.

BEFORE YOU START . . .

Before deciding to sell my own home, I had never used a paintbrush in my life (except in grade school to draw pictures). I'm a doctor, not a home repair person.

The more closely I looked at my house, the more I wanted to improve certain things. I wanted to repaint the recreation room, two bedrooms and the laundry room. I wanted to replace indoor-outdoor carpeting, put up more shelving units, and so on.

I soon exhausted the patience of two friends, who had already painted my kitchen and bathroom. If I wanted additional changes I would have to do them myself. I had a dreadful fear of making the house look worse than it already did, so I was reluctant to proceed.

Quite unexpectedly, I had an opportunity to show the house. Although the house wasn't perfect, I didn't want to miss out on a potential sale. I didn't sell the house. Maybe the improvements would not have made any difference to the buyer, but my embarrassment throughout the ordeal overwhelmed my fear of beginning my home improvement projects.

The next day I got started, and didn't quit until I was satisfied that the house looked as good as I could make it. The lesson? *If I can paint, you can paint.* Do whatever you need to do to give you peace of mind when you eventually show the house.

I will present a brief description of how to improve the various rooms in your house, as well as the front and back yard. This description is far from exhaustive. Much greater detail can be obtained from home decorating books.

My goal is not to turn you into an interior or exterior decorator, but to teach you how to see your home in perspective—to see it as others will, and to prepare the house accordingly. You want to create an atmosphere in which potential buyers can picture themselves living in your home, and to remove all obstacles that interfere with this mood.

Creating a house that buyers want to own should be the essence of all your work. This is much easier to accomplish if the house is clean, in good repair, and free of offending odours or sights, such as a pile of used lumber in the backyard.

While you're waffling over what colour to repaint your kitchen, well-meaning friends will regard you with astonishment. Believe it or not, they might suggest that you forego the paint job, since the new owners will change the colour, no matter how attractive you believe it to be. Regardless of any improvement you want to make, your friends may discourage you, using the same rationale.

It has been my experience that, if you want to paint, then you should paint. It is not their house, but yours. Your friends are trying to help, but when you're ready to show the house, your frame of mind is of utmost importance. Don't leave the slightest doubt about something in your home, like a leaky faucet or dingy laundry room. If you do, you'll want to cringe with embarrassment when prospective buyers arrive at that part of the house. That leaky faucet will haunt you. It will be the albatross around your neck. It will distract you and diminish your sense of confidence—all for the sake of a new washer, or a $25 gallon of paint.

Even if someone buys your house, hates all the new paint and indoor-outdoor carpeting, and starts all over, you'll feel better about showing and selling your home.

If you're ashamed of some part of your home, you won't be able to convey it's true worth to a potential buyer, and will end up losing a fair profit. Do whatever improvements are necessary to give you the ability to sell with confidence and pride in your product—your home.

Consider each room in your home separately.

LAUNDRY ROOM BLUES

Laundry rooms are as underrated as kitchens are overrated, which is why I chose the laundry room as my starting point. Most people think of the laundry room as a second-class part of the house. They always make sure that door is closed when company comes to visit. They whisk buyers quickly through the laundry room when they come to look at the house.

This view is shared by many. How many books are devoted to improving the laundry room? I have yet to see one. However, you can find dozens on improving the kitchen, bathroom, and living room.

A laundry room is a real asset in a home. It offers convenience, privacy and space. If you've ever had to resort to public laundromats or apartment washers and dryers, you'll appreciate what a nuisance it is to spend half the day lugging heavy bags back and forth and waiting for the clothes to be ready.

Compared to a kitchen, expenditures required to improve the look of a laundry room are minimal, and well rewarded.

Objective: Like a kitchen, a laundry room is a working room. This is where people wash, dry, fold and iron clothes. Adequate lighting, room to move about, and a storage area are essential. Homeowners spend a significant amount of time using this room, so it's worthwhile to make it look cheerful.

A Window Is a Real Plus: In a room where you need to inspect clothing, natural light is a real advantage. If you have a window in your laundry room, highlight it. Ensure maximum light, by giving the window a thorough washing. Find a brightly-coloured curtain to draw attention to the window. If the trim needs painting, get to it.

Make It Bright: Ironing and folding are boring in themselves, without having to look at dull, dingy walls. Remember, this is a room where you make things clean,; therefore the room itself should reflect cleanliness. Would you like to cook in a drab, poorly-lit kitchen? The same holds true for the laundry room. Why not make the laundry room inviting? Get out the paint and roller. Choose a light colour. Afterwards, notice how the new paint better reflects the light, and makes the room appear brighter and larger.

Like a cook preparing food, you need adequate lighting to clean and press clothing. Splurge on one or two hundred-watt bulbs and see the difference. If the lighting is still poor, you may consider adding a fluorescent light panel, which you can buy in a self-contained kit, not involving any rewiring.

Add Storage: Take a look at the walls in the laundry room. Is there any room to add a few inexpensive shelves? Storage space in a laundry room is highly desirable. You need some handy place to put your detergents, and other odds and ends (like your laundry).

Maximize Space: Most laundry rooms are small. Have you been using this room as a catch-all area? Are there items, such as spare tires, paint, leftover lumber, storm windows or boxes, that you can remove? Be brutal. If it doesn't have to stay, get rid of it. Why make a small room look even smaller by crowding it with items that aren't essential to the functioning of the room?

Add a Clothesline: Do you have an indoor clothesline? During the cold winter months, it's convenient to have a clothesline to hang delicate articles or freshly pressed clothes. A clothesline also takes advantage of unused space.

Add Colour: How about adding a dash of colour, to create a warm, cheerful atmosphere in a sterile room. A bright red laundry hamper and a few matching storage bins can make a stark room come alive. How about a splashy scatter rug? These are inexpensive items, which you take with you when you leave.

Final Touches: The walls look clean and bright. The lighting is greatly improved. The window is appealing. All the non-essentials have been removed, and the rooms appears larger.

What about the floor? Is the paint chipped, cracked or peeling off? If the floor is tiled, are they in good order? You can inexpensively repaint the floor with a magnificent result. This makes the room look even larger and more finished.

Are the furnace and water heater in this room? If so, make sure you have removed clutter around them, so that buyers have walking space to easily inspect their condition. Give these a good dusting. I painted my furnace ducts white, to match the walls. The ducts had previously been painted a dusty rose, which now only looked dusty. The results looked good, even for an amateur. Have you changed the furnace filter this year?

Now, take a look at the final result. Do you still feel embarrassed by the condition of your laundry room?

THE CLASSIC KITCHEN

Nowadays, there is no such thing as a classic kitchen. Numerous books and magazines devoted exclusively to kitchen design and improvement attest to this fact. Homebuyers have their own ideas of what constitutes the perfect kitchen. This is certainly one room of the house where you can't please everyone. That's not to say that you shouldn't make the most of what you have, but don't spend a fortune trying to impress buyers.

Although it's very easy to overextend your budget improving the kitchen, getting it ready for show does not mean you have to undertake major renovation.

Objective: The kitchen is a working room, a popular, heavy-traffic area. Homeowners eat, bake cookies, can vegetables, drink coffee, wash dishes, read the paper and so on in this room. Cleanliness, spaciousness, handy storage, good working surfaces, and adjustable lighting are critical.

Clean Fresh Look: You can't spend too much time cleaning your kitchen, prior to showing the home. Washing appliances, wiping down light switch plates, and shining the chrome on all the fixtures will be well worth the effort.

Make it immaculate. Take great pains to ensure that this room is clean. People cook and eat here. No one wants to look at, or live with, a grimy sink or stained countertop.

Take a good look at what you've been living with. Does the paint on the walls look a bit tired or soiled? Does it match cupboards and countertops? Perhaps more than in any other room, a fresh coat of light-coloured paint in the kitchen will create an image of freshness and cleanliness.

Lighting: Adequate lighting in a kitchen is an absolute

necessity. You have to be able to see what you're doing. Make sure any broken bulbs are replaced. Many kitchens have adjustable lighting for cooking and dining. If your kitchen is so equipped, be sure to demonstrate this feature, when it comes time to show the house. Although I preferred to show the kitchen with softer illumination, I always took a moment to maximize the lighting, to reassure buyers that they would be able to cook or perform minor surgery in the kitchen without difficulty.

Ventilation: Like lighting, adequate ventilation in a kitchen is important. If you have an exhaust fan or stove hood, point this out when showing the house. It may seem like a small point, but if you've ever lived in a house without a kitchen fan, I'm sure you'll remember greasy, grimy walls and ceilings. To say nothing of smoke fumes from burning food, or toxic fumes from burning plastic.

Storage Space: Potential buyers often like to look in the cupboards, to check for lazy Susans and for total storage space. Take the time beforehand to clean and reorganize them. Cluttered, overcrowded cupboards give the impression of inadequate storage space, even if they are of standard size.

Modern cupboards are a real bonus, but if you have decent cupboards, now is not the time to think of replacement. Such major renovations should be undertaken at the outset of the home purchase, so that you have a chance to enjoy them yourself. Had I made such an investment, for the sole purpose of selling the house, I would have felt devastated to hear potential buyers criticize the style or type of wood. Remember, taste in cupboards, as well as in kitchens, is highly personal. You can perk up older cupboards with fresh paint and posh-looking new door handles.

Surface Areas: Check countertops. Are there appliances, like that worn out toaster-broiler oven, that would best be put away for now?

Don't hide everything, but display only your best. You can make a countertop look uncluttered without creating a sterile appearance. After all, this is a working room. You're still expected to be cooking and eating while you're selling the house. This is hard to do if you don't have any equipment.

Add Some Charm: How about displaying a few sprays of flowers. These look great in a kitchen, and add a flash of colour. All natural. It's an appealing contrast to have modern equipment, like microwave ovens and food processors, and something as warm and charming as a few flowers in a woven basket.

Create a pleasant mood in your kitchen. Clean, efficient and cozy.

THE BEDROOM: TONING IT DOWN . . . WARMING IT UP

Objective: This is the room in which people relax, sleep, read a good book and get dressed. You use this room as a refuge from life's stresses. It should appear spacious, warm and inviting.

The bedroom is the most personal and private room of a house. When you prepare a bedroom for show, understate your personal life by removing items that could embarrass or offend buyers. Even though you think that picture of the nude is attractive, put it away for now.

Stay Away From The Wild Side: Now is not the time to experiment. Even though you think that a mirror on the ceiling might appeal to an adventurous couple, forget it. Keep your ideas mainstream. Save the more colourful changes for your new house.

If you're going to make changes, appeal to as wide an audience as possible. Don't limit your luck.

Space and Illusion: Space is important. When buyers look at bedrooms, the first question they ask is whether or not their antique dressers or queen-sized waterbed will fit. If someone has a seven by seven waterbed, and the bedroom is eight by ten feet, this is going to be an impossible squeeze. You can't change the existing dimensions of the room, but you *can* make the most of what you have. Remove unnecessary furniture, or odds and ends that give the room a cluttered appearance. Clean, organize and remove anything in the closets that you can live without, for now.

Decor: Create a soft, relaxing mood. Hang attractive, simple curtains. Decorate the bed with an elegant bedspread, pillow covers and a few cushions. Throw in a new scatter rug. Light should be subtle, but adjustable for dressing or reading. Add a few flowers for scent and colour.

The bedroom is the most personal and private room of the house. Make it peaceful.

THE LIVING ROOM

Traditionally, the living room has been regarded as the show room, in which you formally entertain guests. Although it may be cozy, this room does not usually have the casualness of the recreation or family room.

As part of my preparation for the living room, I moved my television, VCR, and futon downstairs to the recreation room. Although there was no harm in leaving the furniture where it was, I thought such items would be better suited to the recreation room. Not that I do much high-level entertaining, but this is important to some potential buyers.

The same principles for preparing other rooms apply to the living room. Ensure cleanliness. If walls need painting, paint. Give the carpet a thorough shampooing, for a fresh look and clean odour. If you have a fireplace, clean it out, including scouring down the bricks if they're stained from smoke.

Display only your best furniture and lamps. If you can do without some furniture, put it in storage or give it away. Create an image of spaciousness.

Overall impression: understated, yet respectable. Simple, yet elegant. As always, immaculate.

THE BATHROOM

Like the kitchen, taste in bathrooms is personal. However, most buyers are more flexible about what they will tolerate in a bathroom.

Objective: The bathroom should not only be clean, it should sparkle. Shine the chrome, bleach the floor, scour and polish the sink, toilet and tub. No one wants to inspect a bathroom that is not hygenically presentable. All fixtures should be in top working condition.

If the faucet drips, fix it. If the toilet leaks, or makes noise, fix it. Some buyers flush toilets and run taps to check their condition. Don't neglect repairs that may embarrass you when you're showing the house.

Unless you're prepared to undertake major projects, such as replacing cabinets and redoing tiles, see what can be done simply, and at minimal cost. Paint is cheap. Although elegant matching towels, rugs and shower curtains are not, at least you can take these with you, once the house is sold. Such items add a finished, colour-coordinated touch.

Is the lighting adequate? Again, the bathroom is a high-light-intensity area. At six in the morning, while you're shaving, you like to see what you're doing.

What about the overall condition of the fixtures and plumbing? Do the bathtub tiles need grouting? If yes, do it. Make the bathroom workable, as well as appealing.

Ventilation: As in the kitchen, ventilation in a bathroom is a real plus. If you have an exhaust fan, be sure and point out this feature when you show the house.

Space: Although many bathrooms are smaller than the ideal, there is not much you can do without spending a small fortune to renovate. Maximize existing space. If you can add one or two elegant towel racks or shelves, this will create storage space, without taking up much room. Don't neglect the closet, if you have one. Make it the epitome of organization.

The Half or Three-Quarter Bath: Do you have a half or three-quarter bath? A second bathroom in a home is a definite asset. These special rooms are often ignored. Take a closer look. Once the room is clean and in working order, add a few elegant towels, soaps and simple floral arrangements to make a half bath more appealing.

OTHER ROOMS

Regardless of which room you want to improve (recreation room, den, sewing room), apply the same preparation principles.

It isn't necessary to disguise or hide your television set in the recreation room. After all, this is a family room, designed for such casual entertaining. Ensure that the room is neat, and presentable. It's all right to admit to the fact that, yes, you are actually living in one or two rooms of the house.

THE FRONT YARD

Objective: Make it the best on the block!

Why is the appearance of the yard so important? Before a buyer steps into your house, the first thing he or she sees is the front yard. The front yard forms a critical part of a buyer's first impression of your home. Make it the best it can be.

Landscaping, and general appearance of the front yard say a lot about the homeowner. A well-maintained yard is the result of conscientious, consistent work. Buyers realize you can't make a lawn rich and green overnight. If you take good care of the yard, many buyers will assume that you probably take similar pains to keep the house maintained.

Landscaping: Landscaping is expensive, but highly desirable. If you're fortunate enough to have attractive landscaping, keep it maintained. Remember what you thought of your front yard when you first saw it. Were you impressed? Or was it a new home, begging for some trees, shrubs and bushes?

New homes are a turn-off for many buyers. The yard is sterile, with no greenery for character or shade. The house looks as if it was plunked in an open field or gravel pit.

There's no life surrounding the house. Landscaping a lot is not an overnight project. Even if you pay a small fortune, it takes a few years for new trees and shrubs to "take," and look as though they belong, instead of just being stuck in the ground.

The original landscaping of my home made me want to have a much closer look at the inside of the house. The area in which I lived was like a desert—a few impoverished trees, dirt, dust, hot, dry wind, tumbleweeds, no lakes or hills. I drove by this house and thought it was an oasis. The former owner had obviously taken great pains to create this miniature Garden of Eden. I am an "outdoor" person. Nothing makes me happier than sitting in the backyard in the morning, having a coffee before going to work (where I am stuck indoors for hours). I found the appeal of the yard, both back and front, a tremendous draw. Many buyers feel the same way. They won't mind spending extra money to buy a beautifully landscaped house, because it will give them hours of enjoyment. Don't neglect your front and back yards. Although the house itself is important, it's a mistake to underestimate the value of trees.

The Lawn: Take a critical look at your lawn. Is it plush and green? Is it evenly trimmed? Are there weeds or crabgrass? How does it compare with the neighbours'?

Make your lawn look like a golf course. Water as frequently as necessary to ensure a rich colour. Fertilize as necessary to obtain an even growth. Remove all weeds. Trim borders neatly. Your efforts will be well rewarded.

The Walkway: Ensure that your walkway is as tidy as possible. Sweep away dirt. Remove any garden tools or children's toys when buyers come to visit.

The Entrance: Take a closer look at your front porch. Are there any noticeable signs of aging or lack of maintenance? Is indoor-outdoor carpeting in good condition? Are handrails secure and rust-free? If not, fix up what needs to be done. Something as simple as replacing worn indoor-outdoor carpeting will instantly spruce up an entranceway.

THE BACK YARD

The back yard is where most people relax and entertain during the summer months. Do you have a patio? Or a garden? A clothesline? A fruit tree? A driveway or garage? A storage shed?

Although by no means a gardener, I spent many hours getting my backyard ready for show. As in the front yard, I maintained the lawn, and prepared a flower garden with simple, quick-growing, colourful plants, including petunias, marigolds and geraniums. Weeding isn't much fun, but if you want the yard looking its best, it has to be done.

Driveway: Are there any improvements you can make to your driveway? Are weeds sticking out anywhere? Remove them. Are the edges of the driveway neatly trimmed or bordered? Could the driveway stand an extra load of fresh gravel, or a new coat of blacktop?

Fencing: Check the condition of your fence. Although repairing or replacing a fence is an expensive undertaking, the results are usually breathtaking.

Patio: How about the patio? This should look cozy and inviting. Maximize potential space by getting rid of clutter, such as unused flower pots, garden tools, and empty containers.

Do you have attractive patio furniture? An outdoor table and a few chairs create a pleasant atmosphere, making it easier for potential buyers to see themselves sitting in your backyard, grilling a few steaks on the barbeque.

Additional Considerations: Consider the overall appearance of the back yard. Do you have other appealing features, such as a storage shed or an outdoor clothesline? Do you have any fruit trees, lilac bushes, perennial flowers, such as peonies or lilies of the valley? Even if these plants are not in blossom, make mention of them to visiting buyers.

Is the outdoor lighting adequate for nighttime use? If not, you might want to invest in some inexpensive patio lights.

Are you making the best use of your space? Get rid of any clutter. Leftover pieces of lumber, battered furniture and old paint cans are not attractive. Eliminate everything that makes the yard look smaller or less appealing.

An attractive yard speaks well of the owner. It looks as though you really care about the place. A well maintained lawn is one of the few visible signs (from the street) that here lives someone who is proud of his or her home. Wouldn't you rather buy from someone who has put time and care into her home?

If the body and interior of a used car are in beautiful condition, it's easier to assume that the engine is also in good shape. The same holds true for a house.

DON'T BE CAUGHT OFF GUARD!

Before You Sell, Ensure the Following:

1. Overall appearance of house is good.
2. Foundation is solid.
3. Furnace and water heater are in working order.
4. Adequate wiring and electrical outlets.
5. No water stains in the basement.
6. Work arcas are well-lit.
7. Sewer system is in good condition.
8. Ensure adequate water pressure.
9. Eavestroughs and roof in good repair.
10. Know the size of your water heater.
11. Fireplace and damper in working order.
12. Know your taxes, heating and utility costs.
13. Ensure chimney has no defects.
14. Flooring throughout house in good repair.
15. Paint throughout house looks reasonable.
16. Inform buyers of any major renovations or repairs you have made to the house.

If you do not have time to make repairs, notify buyers in advance of any outstanding flaws, such as faulty wiring.

Chapter Summary

1. If you want top dollar for your house, make all improvements that are necessary to make it worth the asking price.

2. Take the time to look at your house objectively. See what needs to be fixed, or painted, and do it.

3. Well-meaning friends will see you sweating during the preparation of your house for show. They may discourage you from making the effort, by rationalizing that the new owners will change everything to suit their personal taste. Ignore this advice. Listen to your conscience. If something bothers you, fix it. Otherwise, it will haunt you when you actually do show the house.

4. Consider the cost-effectiveness of major renovations, such as replacing kitchen cupboards. Unless you can recover these costs in the selling price, it's not worth the time or expense to undertake such projects.

5. Buyers always check cupboards and closets for storage space, so clean and organize ahead of time. Messy cupboards look much smaller than those that are neat.

6. Space is valuable. Maximize what you have. Eliminate *all* unnecessary furniture, boxes, containers, paint cans, lumber, toys and so on, from both house and yard.

7. Take great pains to thoroughly clean the house. Shampoo carpets, wash or paint walls, wax floors, wipe down wall switch covers, etcetera. Your efforts will be greatly rewarded.

8. Open windows to get rid of unwanted odours. If you

have carpets or floors stained with pet urine, get professional advice. This is a very difficult odour to eliminate.

9. Ensure adequate lighting. Replace broken bulbs. Add a few hundred-watt bulbs to dark hallways, or poorly illuminated rooms, such as the bathroom or laundry room.

10. The appearance of the front yard is critical to a buyer's first impression of your home. Make it the best on the block!

CHAPTER 6

ADVERTISING

It may not be the Taj Mahal, but it's yours. How do you create public interest? How do you get strangers to feel the same way you did, when you bought your house?

Advertise!

The key to successful advertising is to present your product realistically. You have to distance yourself from your home, and regard it as a product for sale.

Before you place your ads, you should be ready to show your house. All repairs should be made, the home spotless and, most of all, your mind should be made up as to the asking price. If you are not prepared, you are not ready to advertise. Advertising is the last step, not the first.

Know your product. Good advertising is the presentation of the product in a form that will attract customers, and screen inappropriate buyers.

DESIGNING THE AD

How do you compose your ad? Take a closer look at the

classified section of the newspaper, to get an idea of the length, content and basic style of house ads. If you decide to take advantage of the free market analyses provided by real-estate companies, most will include a brief summary of the house. If you obtain three market analyses, you should have three written summaries. Compare them, leave in what sounds good and change what you don't like. At least it gives you a starting point.

Or, you can start from scratch. Of course, you've done a complete tour through your house, as well as the front and back yards. Make a list of the attractive features. If necessary, you can go to the local city hall or registry office to obtain core information about your home (accurate structural information, lot size, wiring, number and size of rooms, and so on), which you can use to construct the ad.

THE NEWSPAPER AD

A closer look at good newspaper house ads shows that they all contain some basic information. For example;

> PRIVATE SALE; Cozy 2 plus 1 bedroom bungalow close to STI, attractively landscaped, natural fireplace, asking $151,900, 6 X 6 ft. Jacuzzi optional. Call 693-4516 after 6pm or 694-2463.

This typical ad can be broken into a number of components. These include:

Type of house (bungalow, two storey, semi-detached),
Number of bedrooms,
General location (northwest, downtown, rural),
Proximity to conveniences (walking distance to downtown shopping, close to bus routes, close to public school, nearby parks). No home is an island. Location

is an important consideration for most buyers, for both personal reasons and resale value.
Special features (natural fireplace, underground sprinklers, heated garage, central air conditioning, R-2000 home).
Information as to how and when to get in touch with vendor (call 748-1123 after 5:00 pm or weekends).

These items are standard ad information. Optional information that you might include in the ad would be;

Lot size—only if you have a large lot. Otherwise, you'll pay to advertise the fact that you have a less-than-desirable feature about your home.

House size—only if you have a large house. Why spend money to promote the fact that you have a tiny house?

Construction—brick, stucco, cedar.

Spccific room size—only if you have an exceptional room, such as a large, cleverly-designed kitchen that would appeal to many buyers. Why draw attention to the ordinary?

Condition of home—(newly decorated, immaculate, finished basement, custom-built, updated wiring and plumbing).

Lifestyle—(starter home, ideal for large family, retirement home, "say goodbye to apartment life and hello to a new home of your own," excellent location for owner-rental).

Reason for sale—("owners have purchased another home").

Extra income—(cheaper than rent, rental income—up to $1,200 per month, make money when you sell this 3+1 bdrm home).

Drastically reduced—include *only* if your home is drastically reduced.

Financing conditions—(only when attractive—e.g., vendor will hold mortgage).

Knock 'em dead statements—("a Christmas gift," "unstack the kids," "unbelievable," "super location," "look no more"). Leave the hype to the real estate people. That is, unless you do have a super location or an unbelievable house. Be prepared to deliver what you promise in your ad, or bear the wrath of the perturbed buyer.

SPECIAL CIRCUMSTANCES

The Handyman Special

You want to sell your home, but you don't have time to make it picture-perfect. Hold off calling a realtor. You have a genuinely hot item—a "do-it-yourselfer." Many people are looking for a house that they can fix up. Some buyers want a home, but cannot afford to pay full price for a dolled-up house. They don't mind getting their hands dirty and fixing up a house themselves. Some buyers want a handyman special, so that they can renovate according to their own specifications. They can afford a more expensive home, but would rather spend the savings to redo the house to suit their unique tastes. Or, a buyer wants a house strictly for investment purposes. Unless you're offering a beautiful home for a real bargain price, these buyers will consider only the handyman special. They want to turn the purchase of your house into a profit.

So, if your house is not at its best, advertise as such. You may be surprised at the response. However, be prepared to take this into account when you set your asking price.

For Sale by Owner

By all means, include this as part of your ad. "For sale by owner" or "private sale" are magical drawing cards to your home. It's a real bonus to advertising and selling your home, and one that a real-estate agency cannot provide. Potential buyers know you do not have to pay a realty commission, and expect to negotiate a better deal when they buy from you than they would through a real-estate agent.

KEEP IN MIND

1. Your ad should contain sufficient information to accurately describe the house.

2. Your ad should contain sufficient information to screen inappropriate buyers. Even if you have the most beautiful four-bedroom sidesplit with a built-in pool, a young couple, interested in a starter home, will not want to waste time looking at your house, except maybe to drool. But drooling doesn't sell a home.

3. Understate, rather than overstate, your ad. Don't promise more than you can deliver. An ad blown out of proportion may get people over to look at your house, but that's all. You don't want buyers to feel disappointed or critical when they look at your house. Leave them pleasantly surprised.

As suggested by Russell Oddy (*For Sale By Owner*), if you don't mind taking a gamble, leave an important feature out of your ad and use this as your ace in the hole, when buyers come by to look. ("I didn't know this home had central air conditioning.") However, this tactic is not for the faint of heart.

4. Include the asking price in the ad.

Time and time again, I see private sale ads in the newspaper that do not mention the price. "Why not?" I ask myself. Do the vendors think they'll get a higher price if they don't include it in the ad? Do they want to entice buyers to see the home first, so they can then convince them that it's actually worth the exorbitant asking price?

Not mentioning price in an ad is a drawback. Don't dramatize your ad by adding mystery. No one has time to play this kind of game. You're not unveiling a prize painting. You're selling a product.

The ad is the first place to commit yourself. The asking price is not necessarily the selling price. "But I don't want my nosy neighbours to know what price I'm asking," is no excuse. If neighbours want to find out, they will. By the time you place your ad, you must know your asking price. Otherwise, when buyers start calling, you'll look foolish and disorganized. You're trying to conduct business. Act like a professional.

If you neglect to include the asking price in the ad, you'll find yourself innundated with calls like;

Buyer: I read in the paper that your house is for sale.
Seller: Yes, that's correct. What would you like to know about the house?
Buyer: How much are you asking?

Seller: $96,900.
Buyer: Thank you. 'Bye.

or;

Buyer: I understand that your house is for sale.
Seller: Yes it is. I can fill you in on all the details.
Buyer: How much are you asking for it?
Seller: I'd rather not discuss it over the phone. How about coming over to have a look and we can talk it over then?
Buyer: I'll think it over. Thanks.

You'll never hear from this person again. No one wants to bother. Look at the newspaper ads. If you live in a metropolitan area, you'll see dozens of homes similar to yours for sale. Put yourself in the buyer's position. It's a real zoo out there. Would you waste time phoning all the ads, just to find out the asking price? Buyers like to be practical. Even if your home is a palace, there's no point in showing it to someone who can't afford it. Save yourself time. Be considerate of the buyer's time.

Most ads sound alike. The ad does *not* sell your home. The home sells itself. You want to attract customers. This is the purpose of the ads, to get people to call you and come over for a look.

Placing an ad without including the asking price is like fishing without a lure. With so many people fishing in the same pond at the same time, who's going to get the nibble? Take a stand. Give the asking price.

THE ADDRESS

For purposes of advertising, I suggest including general location, but not the specific address. Most buyers have some idea, if not a very specific idea, of the area of town in which they would like to live. Giving the general location serves to describe your property, and will attract those who wish to live there and screen those who do not. People need to know for obvious reasons—to be near schools and parks for children, to be within walking distance of work, shopping, worship and recreation facilities. Others consider the neighbourhood for lifestyle and resale value.

If you mind strangers driving slowly past your house at all hours to have a look, don't include the specific address. If they are serious buyers they'll phone you for the address. They will also understand why you haven't included this information in the ad. Although selling a home is public, it's in your best interest to keep some aspects out of a newspaper advertisement. You want to attract serious buyers—not curiosity seekers.

By stating the general location, you'll get appropriate callers. It's a valuable screening device.

THE LAWN SIGN

Whether or not to display a *For Sale* sign on your front lawn is a controversial matter. Some feel that this is an excellent form of free advertising. Using a lawn sign is thought to be a good way to attract buyers who happen to be driving through your neighbourhood. It announces to neighbours, who may tell their friends, that you're selling your home. No one can argue with these valid reasons.

I did not use a *For Sale* sign. My privacy was more important than this form of advertising. I was not prepared to put up with unexpected strangers showing up at the door, lured by the lawn sign. I was living on my own, and preferred to have tight control of access to my house.

Granted, I may have missed out on some legitimate customers, but I was willing to sacrifice this business for peace of mind.

The choice is yours. If you do opt for a lawn sign, make it look professional. You can buy *For Sale by Owner* signs in most stationery stores. Include your name, phone number, and the hours during which buyers are welcome to look through the house. For example;

FOR SALE BY OWNER
J. Smyth (224-5456)
Open for viewing nightly
7:00-9:00 p.m. or call for appt.

WHERE TO ADVERTISE

I've spoken at length about newspaper advertising. You should also take advantage of opportunities for free advertising. These include bulletin boards at community centres, supermarkets, and public buildings (e.g., universities).

Don't underestimate word-of-mouth advertising. I told everyone I knew that I was selling my home. Talk is cheap, but you never know. That friend of a friend of a friend might be the very person who ends up buying your home.

WHEN TO ADVERTISE

Which days of the week are best to advertise? Some say the Sunday paper, because that's the day most people like to look at houses. Others say Thursday or Friday to get weekend shoppers. I think the most important thing is to advertise on those days when you're sure you can be available for showing the home. Should you advertise daily for one or two weeks? Should you advertise for three days at a time? I don't think there's any perfect answer. But I do know that there's no point in paying for a newspaper ad if you cannot be at home to answer calls.

AVAILABILITY

This is crucial. You must make yourself available if you want to sell your home. Nothing is more frustrating to an interested buyer than being unable to follow up your ad. This doesn't mean you have to become a phone slave twenty-four hours a day. You can state in your ad "call after 6:00 p.m." or whenever you'll be available to take calls. But once you commit yourself in writing—be home. If it's not too disruptive, give your work number as well. This will ensure that you're not likely to miss calls from people who work shifts, or are otherwise unavailable during the evening.

Chapter Summary

1. The purpose of the ad is to draw clients to see your home—not to actually sell the house.

2. A well-designed ad should simultaneously attract potential buyers and screen inappropriate calls.

3. Describe your home accurately.

4. Understate, rather than overstate, your ad. Leave clients pleasantly surprised, rather than disappointed, when they see the house—don't promise the moon, if all you have is the cheese.

5. No house is an island. If you're near shopping areas, schools, churches or parks, include this in your ad.

6. Include the general location, but not the specific address.

7. Unless you have an outstanding house or lot size, leave these particulars out of the ad. Don't pay to advertise your home's weak points.

8. Include *For Sale by Owner*, or *Private Sale* in the ad. This is a genuine drawing card and one that a real-estate agent cannot provide.

9. Include your phone number (and work number, if appropriate) and state a time for buyers to call (e.g. call after 5:00 p.m.).

10. Be available for receiving phone calls when your ad specifies.

11. Avoid using hard-sell words like "bargain of the year," "best deal ever," or "get rich beyond your wildest dreams," unless you are prepared to follow through on your promise.

12. If you don't have time to fix up your home, advertise it as a handyman special, and lower your price accordingly. You'll still make a profit.

13. Include your asking price in the ad.

14. Take advantage of free advertising opportunities.

15. Give your ads a chance to work—at least four weeks.

CHAPTER 7

THE FIRST CONTACT—THE TELEPHONE

The purpose of the telephone contact is to encourage buyers to have a look at your house. The telephone conversation, in itself, does not sell your house.

Your telephone conduct has some bearing on the number of buyers you'll have viewing the house. This section discusses how to handle yourself while on the phone with buyers.

BE PREPARED:

Be at Home—If your ad says "call after 5:00 p.m.," be at home to receive calls. Although this is common sense, some people take buyers for granted. "I'm just stepping out for some groceries—if they really want the house, they'll call again."

If you need extra time after work to run errands, adjust your ad accordingly; "call after 6:00 p.m.," or "call after 7:00 p.m.," then *stay at home*.

Most serious buyers believe a good house will sell fast. They don't waste time calling. If you don't show up until 9:00 p.m., most buyers will have already given up on your house. You've made a committment. Stick to it. Otherwise, don't advertise, because you're not ready to sell.

Make It Simple—If more than one person shares the household, designate one or two people *only* to handle calls related to your ad. This will prevent confusion.

Be Consistent—Be organized. As suggested by Oddy, prepare a list of "house facts" to keep by the phone, to help you answer questions quickly and accurately.

As a guideline, this list should contain the following minimum facts about your home;

Age of home,
Type of construction,
Lot size,
House size,
Number of bedrooms,
Property taxes,
Type of heating (hydro, oil),
Plumbing (age, copper),
Insulation (type, amount),
Amperage, and
Proximity to schools, parks, shopping etc.

Expect Standard Questions—Be prepared for questions relating to lot size, age of house, house size, property taxes, and the address.

Volunteer Your Reason for Selling—If your reasons for selling are unrelated to negative aspects of the home, don't be shy about telling buyers why you're selling. "I really hate to sell, but I have a new job in another province." This reassures buyers you aren't trying to sell them a lemon.

Discourage Nosiness—Be wary of someone who asks 1,001 questions. This kind of person is either very interested or simply nosy (a neighbour or real-estate agent).

Callers don't need to know if you're selling the washer and dryer with the house. They don't need to know how much of your mortgage remains to be paid off.

Identify genuine callers by inviting them to have a look at the house. An uninterested party will always decline this offer.

Always Be Polite—You may not know with whom you're speaking—and it really doesn't matter. Courteous behaviour reflects professionalism.

Be Friendly—This is your first contact with a potential buyer. It's a big step for them to visit your home. After all, you're a stranger. Put yourself in the buyer's position. If the owner sounds cold or too "hard sell" on the phone, would you go out of your way to look at his or her house? Answer questions fully. Thank interested parties for their call. Encourage buyers to call again or, better yet, to drop by for a look.

Don't Monopolize Phone Time with One Caller—Don't discourage other calls by spending too much time with one person. Newspaper ads don't sell homes. Neither do initial phone calls. The purpose of the call is to get people to look at your house.

Limit each call to a maximum of ten minutes. Interested callers will probably take much less time.

Discourage family members from tying up the phone with personal calls. This annoying habit is frustrating to a buyer who is trying to follow up on your newspaper ad, and he or she may give up.

Invite Them Over—If the caller decides to visit your home, make an appointment at his or her convenience.

At this early, fragile stage, don't create hurdles by limiting visits to see your home only to times that are convenient for you. You're in the business of selling your house. Be considerate and professional. Make it easy for buyers to come over.

Ask for Their Names—If buyers are coming right over to see your house, it doesn't hurt to ask for at least their first names. This prevents confusion, particularly if you have a *For Sale* sign in the front yard, which invites anyone to drop in anytime. Serious buyers will understand and give you their name. If they don't, you'll know they aren't interested in the house.

If a buyer isn't coming over until the next day, ask for both the name and phone number. Should there be any last-minute changes in your schedule, you will have some means of letting the buyer know in advance. Or else, ask buyers to phone prior to their visit.

Do your best to accommodate potential buyers. At this stage, if you can't show the house when it's convenient for others, you aren't ready to sell.

Remember, you have an *interested* party. If you were fishing, you wouldn't give up at the first nibble. Welcome potential buyers to your home with open arms.

Chapter Summary

1. Be at home to receive calls, as stated in your ad. If you can't be home, you're not ready to advertise.

2. Prevent confusion, by having only one or two household members answer calls concerning your ad.

3. Be consistent by being prepared. Compose a list of "house facts" and keep it handy by the phone.

4. Volunteer your reason for selling your house. This will reassure buyers they're not getting a lemon.

5. Be polite, always.

6. Limit calls to ten minutes. A phone call doesn't sell the house.

7. Invite buyers to come over for a visit. Make it at their convenience, not yours.

CHAPTER 8

CLOSE ENCOUNTERS OF THE FOURTH KIND

SHOWING THE PRODUCT

Opening your door to strangers in order to sell your home is probably not part of your day job. Nor is it a typical social activity. This doesn't mean you have to take the easy way out and hire a real-estate agent. Take a deep breath. You've already prepared the home—cleaned, painted, polished and created moods in each room. You've settled on a well-thought-out price. You've advertised successfully. You've strengthened a budding interest, created by your advertisement, by your telephone conduct. Buyers are actually coming over to have a look. So far, everything is going well.

Be prepared for all types of people. You're going public. If you're overly sensitive, put this kind of indulgence on the shelf for a while. Buyers may make comments about your home that are not always complimentary. They may be trying to decide if your home is what they want. Realize that not everyone who drops by will be a serious buyer. maybe one or two are thinking of selling their own home, and want to see what you're offering. Take it in stride. No harm is meant. Welcome to the business world.

You're probably nervous. I certainly was. Remember, buyers are people too, and its possible they might also be nervous. You can and will be able to relate. You've done all the preparation. Now go out there and SELL!

Before you open your door to the first caller, be prepared;

Ensure good illumination throughout the house. Particularly downstairs, or in dim hallways or bathrooms, put lights on *before* viewers arrive.

No surprises. Even though the house might be clean, it doesn't hurt to do a quick check, to ensure that personal items are stored away, counter tops are neat, and all is as you would expect it to be.

No offensive or strong odours. Odours are sometimes difficult to detect if you've been indoors for a period of time. Ventilate rooms by opening doors and windows for ten minutes before visitors arrive. To create attractive smells, some homeowners brew a fresh pot of coffee, but this is not necessary.

Keep your list of "house facts" handy. I kept a few photocopies available for giving out to interested people.

Create the atmosphere for showing. The house should be calm, quiet and controlled. Some people play soft music. I didn't. I wanted buyers to be able to concentrate when they looked through the house. I didn't want any competition from the stereo, or other distractions. Needless to say, if you have enthusiastic pets or children, do your best to keep noise to a minimum.

SHOWING TIPS

AT THE FRONT DOOR

Greet buyers politely—begin by introducing yourself. Offer to take their coats. If they don't remove their footwear, ask them to do so, particularly if it's raining and you have freshly shampooed rugs. At first, I was too inhibited, not wishing to offend a potential buyer before he had his feet in the door. Not only did I not sell the house, but I had an unnecessary mess to clean up afterwards. Not worth it. It's still *your* home.

GIVE THEM THE GRAND TOUR

Some people suggest letting buyers wander through your home on their own. In this manner, buyers will have less pressure and more privacy to discuss aspects of your home.

I disagree. There are a number of considerations to keep in mind when showing your house:

Buyer Expectation

Most buyers *expect you* to come along. After all, that's the way real-estate agents show homes. On their own, buyers might feel even more pressured to go through the house quickly, particularly if they think you're just killing time until they leave. Buyers might interpret your *laissez-faire* attitude as meaning you're not really interested in selling the house. Who knows?

Availability for Questions

As they go through the house on their own, buyers might think of questions they forget to ask you later—or worse yet, they might make incorrect assumptions, damaging to a possible sale. For example, a buyer might assume that your fireplace is fake. If you're giving the tour, you can mention that it's a well-used, natural fireplace with a built-in vent for disposing of ashes.

If you're available, you can answer questions before buyers have a chance to formulate false assumptions.

Stimulus Overload

Going through a new home provides a sudden influx of stimulation. You want to ensure that buyers don't miss the forest for the trees. Without being overbearing, as you go from room to room, you simply point out highlights or special features, custom made drapes, heat lamp in the bathroom, convenient linen closets, lazy Susan, dimmer switches for bedrooms, ventilation fans, and so on.

By the way, please let buyers go through rooms *first*. You'd be amazed how quickly a small bedroom looks even smaller with four people jockeying for position. Make your showing as free of awkwardness as possible.

HELP BUYERS TO FEEL AT HOME

Please touch—please open—please feel free to look and ask questions—*please feel at home*. This is the relaxed atmosphere you should encourage.

DON'T RUSH

It's natural to feel nervous when you first start to show your home. Unfortunately, nervousness makes many people speak quickly, and ramble on and on. Such homeowners give a whirlwind tour of the house, blurting out facts from a piece of paper. Before they realize it, the buyer is already out the door. Far from selling the home, they scarcely recollect what happened—it all went so fast. The buyer feels the same way.

Take your time. Make a conscious effort to appear relaxed and confident as you show the house. Slow down your speech. Each time you show the house this will get easier.

Slowing down benefits both the buyer and yourself. It gives you a chance to learn something about the buyer. When you concentrate on the buyer, you forget about the house. This is what should happen. You've done everything to get the house ready. Sooner or later the right buyer will come along. Now you have to devote your attention to recognizing who this person is. Be receptive to *buying signals* and other messages the buyer is sending. LISTEN TO BUYERS!

MAINTAIN CONTROL

There's a certain psychology to the order in which you show the rooms of your house. Because of the bombardment of stimulation, most buyers have rather short memories. Try this experiment. After completing a tour of your home, ask a buyer to describe the floor in the main bathroom. He or she won't remember. This is natural. You want buyers to remember the best features of your home. Therefore, you direct your house tour to end up in that room.

THE FINESSE OF SHOWING

You want to be professional when you show your home. As you conduct your tour, you have to consider how you conduct yourself. Knowing what to say, when to say it, and how much to say, takes skill and thoughtfulness.

Know Your House Facts Cold

Remember that you're selling your house privately. Quite naturally, most buyers do not feel 100% comfortable with this thought. What if you're trying to sell them an overpriced home? What if the house is about to fall apart?

Although real-estate agents provide no guarantee of honesty and sincerity, they do have their professional reputations at stake. Unlike you, they have more than one home to sell. If they want to stay in business, it's not in their best interests to deliberately misrepresent your house. In addition, most buyers are accustomed to purchasing their homes through a real-estate agent. You have to put some effort into gaining a buyer's confidence.

Know the facts regarding your house. Nothing is more reassuring to potential buyers than homeowners who know what they're talking about. This also separates good real-estate agents from poor ones. Someone who has done her homework on a house and can answer questions quickly and accurately is more likely to put a buyer at ease and in a mood to seriously discuss the house, than someone who is constantly saying "I'm not sure about that. I'll look it up and get back to you." Meanwhile, the buyer has already seen another house and is no longer interested in the lot size of your property.

Getting Caught Off Guard

You're not a computer. It's possible that a buyer might ask you something you aren't prepared to answer. This happened to me. While going through the basement, someone asked me the amperage of the house. I didn't know the answer. (Later, I realized it was on my list of house facts.) This is bound to happen sooner or later, regardless of how well prepared you are. Be truthful. If you don't know something, admit it.

Let Buyers Know Why You Are Selling the Home

I've already discussed this point, but it's worth repeating. Unless you're selling because you can't stand all the problems in the house, tell buyers why you have decided to sell. Particularly since you are selling privately, buyers need reassurance that they aren't buying a lemon. The best way to convince someone that your house isn't a time bomb, is to provide a legitimate reason why you're selling.

Never Apologize for Your Home

Be it ever so humble. . . .

At first, I had to force myself not to do this. Believe it or not, it's natural to feel that you must account for every feature, good or bad, in your house. It's a defence mechanism created by anxiety and lack of confidence. Alternatively, some homeowners feel compelled to exaggerate qualities of the house, to the point where their credibility is seriously in question.

No house is perfect. If you wanted to tear it down and start over again, sure, you could make the entrance foyer just a wee bit bigger. *No one expects your house to be perfect.* Most serious buyers want to fall in love with your house.

Remember when you were looking for a home? Do you recall how painful it was to look at house after house, trying to find something reasonable? After a while, the various features become blurred and you can't remember which house had that really nice kitchen with the built-in range, but also had that small back yard and unfinished basement, with the high taxes. Or was that a difference place?

Most buyers, consciously or unconsciously, walk into your house prepared to accept minor imperfections. That is, unless you talk down the house so much, through nervousness, that you succeed in convincing them that your house is seriously flawed. Even though they liked it enough from the outside to come in and take a closer look.

You can be your own worst enemy. You can talk yourself out of a sale just as easily as you can warm someone up to buying the place.

Never Lie About Your House

If you lie and get caught, you have instantly lost all of your credibility. Even if you don't get caught at the outset, if you've lied about a critical aspect of your home, such as your lot size, the deal will fall apart when it comes time to close.

Lying leaves a very bad taste with most people. Such an action may finish you for selling your own home, unless you live in a major metropolitan area with a never-ending, continually-changing pool of buyers. You will have to resort to a real-estate agency. In such a case, you should consider yourself lucky to have this option available to you.

Don't Give Equal Time to Less Outstanding Features

On the other hand, you don't have to blurt out a ten-page list of every feature of your home that you do not consider outstanding. Answer every question honestly. However, honesty does not require that you give equal time to your home's weakest points. If a buyer mentions that you have a small bedroom and it's true, admit it. But then, remind the buyer that the family room has a natural fireplace with a massive picture window.

Don't Interrupt

This is an extremely annoying habit. If a buyer is trying to make a point and you continually interrupt, you might end up losing a sale. Let buyers speak their piece. It shows they're interested.

Don't Be Aggressive or Pushy

Forget about using a hard-sell approach. If you have to use pressure to sell your home, you're selling to the wrong person. This creates tension and hard feelings, but no sale. Don't try so hard. It won't work. Pushiness stems from insecurity. Deep down, you don't think much of yourself or your home. The only way you think you can sell is to push the house on the first person who makes a positive comment.

Have you ever wandered into an exclusive clothing store and been pounced upon by one or two sales clerks? "Can I help you?" "No thanks, I'm just browsing." Even when they stop, you feel their eyes are boring holes in your back. Doesn't it make you want to leave and go somewhere where you can concentrate on buying? Even though the products in the exclusive store may be of better quality, and more to your liking, you have to shrug off the distractions imposed by the vendors. It's too much like work. Who needs the third degree, when all you want is a sweater?

If the atmosphere is oppressive while showing the home, *you are to blame*, not the buyer. Relax. Believe in your product.

Avoid Shyness

Don't fall into the opposite pattern. Shyness is almost as unprofessional, and even more uncomfortable than a hard-sell approach. At least some buyers can talk down a braggart or an overenthusiastic salesperson. Fear of offending buyers, to the point of paralysis, will overwhelm any chance of a sale.

Remember, you've purchased at least one home. Reverse roles for a moment. How did you feel when you were looking at homes? Anticipate the needs and concerns of the buyer.

Don't Ramble

I have a strong tendency to ramble when I'm nervous. I repeat myself, or mutter on and on about things that the buyer probably doesn't even want to hear. Listen to yourself and STOP TALKING.

Rambling leads to a second serious mistake—volunteering unnecessary information. Buyers will ask you questions that are important to them. If they want to know something, they'll ask. Otherwise, keep your mouth shut and your mind open.

Remember, you can talk yourself *out* of a sale. What you say can be critical. Take your time. Speak clearly. Weigh your words.

You Don't Need a Thesaurus to Sell Your Home

If you aren't accustomed to using ten-dollar words to express yourself, now is not the time to start. Technical jargon won't sell your home, either. Some people use big, unusual words to impress others. Or they use this technique in a feeble attempt to disguise their lack of understanding. You don't need to resort to this behaviour. You want to establish a rapport, not alienate buyers. Be yourself.

Be Polite

There's no excuse for rudeness. Not ever. If someone insults you or your house, ask them to leave. Word quickly gets around. Buyers who might have been better suited for your house won't bother because they've heard you gave their second cousin a hard time, when he was looking at your house last week.

Using the same rationale, never argue with buyers. Stay calm, even if someone says something that's completely incorrect about your house. Wait until the buyer has finished, and fill him or her in on the facts.

Don't Get Bogged Down in Trivia

Even if you know a buyer personally, selling your home is serious business. This is *not* the time to gossip about work or make small talk.

When I was showing my house to buyers, I said very little about myself, exception to mention why I was selling the home (moving out of province). If they asked my occupation, I gave a very general answer: "Oh, I work at the base hospital." The last thing I wanted to make known was that I was a doctor. Somehow, potential buyers drift from the topic of the house and start talking about their various aches and pains.

You're selling your home. Not yourself. Granted, selling is easier if buyers feel welcome and comfortable in your home. This goal is attainable if you make yourself seem approachable, friendly and sincere. But don't overdo it. Strike a balance between cordiality and effusiveness.

When buyers arrive at your home, don't offer coffee or a drink. First, show the house. Answer all questions. Once it's clear that the house matter is settled for the time being, then talk about something else. If you get sidetracked right from the beginning, you'll forget your objective of selling the house. By the time the buyers leave, you might have had a fascinating discussion (albeit about something other than the house), but you haven't come any closer to selling your home.

Listen to Potential Buyers

Even when you think you're so knowledgeable about your house that you could sell it blindfolded with one hand tied behind your back, listening to potential buyers will teach you even more.

I can recall showing my home to three elderly ladies. Throughout my tour, I caught fragments of "oohs" and "ahs" and "nice antiques." However, something else really took me by surprise. I was following them down the stairs to show the basement, when one woman made a comment about the sturdiness of the handrail. I didn't have to be a doctor to appreciate that she had difficulty walking because of a hip problem. Obviously, a safe stairway was important to her—something I had overlooked because it wasn't as important to me.

It was quite a valuable lesson. Fortunately, I was well on my way to mastering the art of letting the house sell itself. If I had kept up a continual barrage of description of the features that *I* thought were salient, I would never have seen my house as those women did.

If you had to sell your house to yourself, it would be easy. Unfortunately, its not that simple.

Concentrate on the Buyers—Forget the House

The value of focusing on buyer needs cannot be overstated.

This requires careful listening. If you want to sell, you have to understand what each person is looking for in a home.

I showed my house to a young couple. While they looked through the place, I noticed they spoke very little to each other. The wife's silence was unnerving, until it dawned on me that she spoke little English. The husband and I had been prattling on at breakneck speed, and she probably felt quite left out and ill at ease. Although not fluent in French, I tried to include her as much as possible. I slowed my speech to a reasonable pace and made frequent eye contact. Using my high school French, I asked her what she thought of the new location. It was easy to tell from her pained expression that she was homesick and badly in need of a cozy home she could call her own. At this point in the tour, I led the buyers to my best feature, the Jacuzzi room. The wife's facial expression gave her away. The unexpected elegance of the room sold her completely on the house. (This was no accident—I worked for hours to create the best mood possible, through a jungle of silk plants and careful light arrangement.) All my efforts were rewarded when I saw her eyes light up. Body language is universal.

Include Everyone

If you're selling a home to more than one person, involve everyone (over the age of sixteen) who comes to look. Concentrating only on one person creates resentment in others. This error is typical of poor salesmen. Consider the situation where a couple walk into a car dealership. Even though the woman is the one buying the car, the salesman addresses only her male companion. I don't know how often this has happened to me, whether I was buying lumber, a computer or car parts. This behaviour is rude and irritating. If I can't get this message through to the salesman quickly enough, I go elsewhere to make my purchase.

If you're oblivious, just plain sexist, or otherwise bigoted in your attitude, it will be your undoing. Acting like an amateur produces similar results. You need to talk directly to everyone, and *always* to the person asking the question.

Unless you're selling to only one person, you have to persuade everyone involved to buy the house. Get support from family members or companions, and let them finish the selling for you. To be successful, you need to have the "significant others" persuade the one with the money to buy the house. *This process starts from the moment they walk in for their first look.*

Be Alert for Buying Signals

Keep your ears open. While showing the house, listen for questions such as: "Are the drapes included?" or, "Are you selling the fridge and stove with the house?" These are signs of an interested buyer. I responded to these types of questions with statements like: "If you're interested, I'm sure we could work something out," or "I'd like to include the drapes as part of the deal because they suit the home and belong with it. Why don't you think it over and make an offer?"

Stay alert. Buying signals present golden opportunities to enhance interest in your home, which will eventually lead to a sale.

The tour is complete. . . .

INVITE BUYERS TO HAVE A SECOND LOOK ON THEIR OWN

If buyers aren't already heading for the front door (assuming they remember where it is), suggest that they have another look on their own. Time permitting, most interested buyers will take a second look. They should be quite relaxed by now and will be better able to assess your home. Taking a second look on their own provides an opportunity for buyers to double-check important features of your home, and to bring these to the attention of their companions. It gives buyers a chance to picture themselves living in your home.

INVITE QUESTIONS

Be friendly and open. Ask buyers if they have any questions. If they seem very interested and in no hurry to leave, invite them to stay for a beverage. (Select the most attractive room in the house for this purpose.) If buyers seem to like the house, but have to leave, ask for their full names, phone number and a good time to call. Before they leave, give them a copy of your house facts, which includes your name and phone number.

Don't feel you haven't done a good job if viewers seem to like the house, but don't stay for coffee. Everyone has a slightly different style. Buying a house is a big decision. (Even one as nice as yours.) Most people need a day or two to make up their minds. They also need to discuss it privately. It would be nice if buyers agreed to make an offer on the spot, but most need a bit of personal space and time. Don't forget, you don't have the benefit of a real-estate agent who can take buyers out to the car and pressure them into immediately putting in an offer.

Let the house sell itself. At times, this can be nerve-racking. You can't appear too eager for a written offer. It looks as though you're desperate. Alternatively, you can't appear too casual, because it looks as if you're not taking a buyer's genuine interest seriously. Being too pushy will scare off most sincerely interested buyers.

If buyers provide you with their names and phone number, and agree to be called in a day or so, they're genuinely interested in buying your home. If they don't want to bother, they are not. It's that simple.

DON'T BE THE FIRST TO MENTION PRICE

If you've advertised properly, buyers will already know your asking price. Focus on the home and its benefits, not the price. Before making an offer, some buyers will bluntly ask for your lowest price. If this happens, repeat your asking price, and invite them to make you an offer. (If your asking price is flexible, you might want to mention it at this time.) You've stated your position. It's now up to them to decide if they want to play ball.

DON'T TAKE ADVANTAGE OF BUYERS

Have confidence in your home. On one occasion, a man told me he wanted to buy my house but didn't know how to go about it. This was during the first showing. He and his wife had not had a chance to talk. This fellow knew my asking price was flexible (within reason, of course). Rather than exploit this hot customer's naivety in not knowing how to make an offer, I suggested that he discuss it further with his wife and get back to me. I'm sure the average real-estate agent would have taken the couple back to the car, and told them to immediately put in an offer.

Buying or selling a house can be a confusing, complicated matter. Don't add additional embellishments before you've established a final price. Earlier, this buyer asked whether certain items were to be included with the sale of the house (buying signals). Rather than haggle over details so early in the deal, I told him I would prefer to wait until he had made an offer, at which time we could discuss the finer points.

I did ask this couple for their names and phone number. I assured them that if someone else wanted the house while they were deciding, I would call before I sold it. In other words, they didn't have to fear that I would sell the house before they had a chance to put in an offer. Real-estate agents thrive on quick sales by doing the opposite. "You'd better put in an offer, because another couple really wants the house, and is planning on putting an offer in tonight. Wouldn't it be a shame to lose the house for a measly $1,000?" I know this is true because it happened to me.

Have some class. If you've got a good house for sale and are asking a reasonable price, you don't have to trick, pressure or con people into buying it.

DON'T UNDERMINE YOUR EFFORTS

There's another side to the business of selling. This is where it starts to get complicated.

Even for a serious buyer, there is resistance to making the final leap into instant debt. Buying a house is still a big deal. Most people need some sort of push before they actually sign on the dotted line. After showing the house, if you leave buyers with the impression they have all the time in the world to make an offer, this is exactly what they'll do.

Too much pressure or a hard sell turns buyers away. However, applying no pressure at all is equally destructive to a sale. If you give buyers the impression you'll wait for ever for an offer, they might feel they are doing you a favour by buying your house (which will be reflected in their eventual offer). As in fishing, if you don't tug on the line from time to time, even the fish gets bored and moves on to a more interesting meal. *No one wants something if no one else wants it.* The value of whatever it is you're trying to sell is diminished if it's not in demand.

Buyers *are* doing you a favour by buying your house, but the bargaining should be on equal terms. They want a good deal. You want a fair price. It's much easier to satisfy both parties if the house is still in demand. I mentioned to my buyers that another person was quite serious about the house (which was true), and of course, I was expecting to hear from him (which I was). Along with everything else, these buyers took this information home with them that night.

BE PROFESSIONAL

When buyers are ready to leave, thank them for coming to look at your house. It's a compliment to your advertising efforts, and to the appearance of your home.

OTHER CONSIDERATIONS

Moral Support

When I first started to show my house, I felt better having a friend present (albeit, in the background, reading the paper). Seeing a familiar face in the house helped me to feel more sure of myself.

However, the presence of friends during the showing of your home can be a double-edged sword. On one occasion, I was showing the house to a mutual acquaintance. Afterwards, while making small talk over coffee, my overzealous friend took it upon herself to ask this potential buyer how to repair some paint chips under the bedroom window. (Previously, we had disagreed about repairing the wall.) She led him to the room to point out the exact site. He inspected the paint chips and said, "Oh, that's from water damage, and its very easy to fix." When this potential buyer first looked at the bedroom, he commented only on the cross-ventilation between the two windows—a feature that seems to be disappearing in new homes. Suddenly, the chipped paint had become the most outstanding feature in the room. He didn't buy the house. Probably the chipped paint had no bearing on his decision but, needless to say, I never invited that friend (or any other friend) over when I was planning to show the house and, yes, I repaired the window and repainted the bedroom.

Open House

Should you or shouldn't you . . .

An open house is exactly what it says. A house open to the public for a period of time, to permit anyone who is interested to drop in and have a look. Visitors do not need an appointment or previous contact with the seller. Open houses are popular selling tools for real-estate agents, for a number of reasons;

> It makes the home owner feel satisfied. It's visible proof that the real estate agent is going out of his or her way to try and sell the house.
>
> It provides free advertising for the particular real-estate agency. WESELLHOMES Realty is having an open house at 224 Oak Street.
>
> It's a valuable marketing tool for the real-estate agent. Many people will drop by to have a look, but are not interested in buying your home. However, the agent has the opportunity to discuss other properties with these potential buyers, and might come closer to selling another property, while he or she is showing your house.

Should you have an open house? Why not? Think about it. Every time a buyer looks at your home, this is, in effect, a scaled-down version of an open house. You've put a great deal of effort into preparing your home for show. There's no harm in maximizing this form of free advertising.

Plan an open house a few days in advance. You might consider advertising in the newspaper. The very least you should do is make up a few "OPEN HOUSE—Sunday 1:00-4:00 p.m." signs. Put one sign on your front lawn, and a second sign at the nearest major road access, with arrows pointing the way to your house.

Keep your expectations realistic. Many people enjoy looking at homes, but are not serious buyers. For many, going to open houses is something to do on a Saturday or Sunday afternoon. Still, you never know. The person that you thought was just looking might be a serious, low-key buyer, who prefers the less pressured atmosphere of an open house.

During an open house, most real-estate agents let buyers wander around on their own, particularly if there are a lot of people in the house. It's the only practical solution. You can afford to be more casual during open house presentations, because buyers expect it to be so, and are less likely to commit themselves if you start trying to pin them down to make an offer.

Keep several copies of "house facts" available. Distribute these throughout the house—the front door, living room coffee table, and an upstairs bedroom dresser. Make the most of your free advertising.

Have fun. An open house is a good opportunity to "break the selling ice," if you've not already done so. Get used to the feeling of strangers wandering through your home.

Even though you may not sell your home, an open house will give you some practice in showing your house, in addition to the free advertising. You never know. Maybe one of those Sunday browsers has a friend who's looking for a home just like yours!

BEFORE YOU SHOW . . .

1. Do a last minute check throughout the house to avoid embarrassing surprises.

2. Be sure that the lights are on, especially in poorly lit areas.

3. Ensure there are no strong or offensive odours. Air the home before visitors drop by.

4. Create an atmosphere for showing—calm and controlled.

5. Keep your list of "house facts" handy. Have a few copies to distribute to potential buyers.

Chapter Summary

1. Be prepared for all types of people.
2. Give a tour yourself, and save the best for last. Then, let buyers have a second look on their own.
3. Help buyers feel at home. Be friendly.
4. Don't rush or ramble.
5. Let buyers know why you're selling the house.
6. Know the facts about your house cold.
7. Never apologize for your house.
8. Never lie.
9. Avoid bragging or exaggeration.
10. Don't use a hard-sell approach. Let the house sell itself.
11. Don't give equal time to less outstanding features.
12. Use clear, simple language to express yourself.
13. Be polite, always.
14. Don't get trapped in trivia.
15. Forget about the house—listen closely to buyers.
16. Invite questions.
17. Don't be the first to mention price.

18. If they appear interested, ask for their names and phone number. Give them a copy of your "house facts."

19. Be professional!

CHAPTER 9

THE PSYCHOLOGY OF SELLING

BASIC SELLING PRINCIPLES

There's no shortage of books on the art of selling. Regardless of whether you are selling encyclopaedias or rocket fuel, the underlying principles are the same.

Be Well Informed About Your Product

Do your homework. Learn everything there is to know about your house. A knowledgable seller inspires a buyer's confidence and trust.

When buyers come by for a look, keep available a clipboard containing house information. Although it would be ideal to memorize this information, it's still better to refer to a list than to fumble for the answer.

Ask a Reasonable Price

This is critical. Even the nicest home becomes unsellable if the asking price is beyond reach. Your goal is to sell the house, not to get rich. Be fair. Otherwise, you may find yourself alone at the bargaining table. Eventually, you'll drop the price in order to sell. If you're realistic from the outset, you'll sell much sooner, and the entire process will be less painful.

Treat the Buyer with Respect

Treating a buyer with respect involves taking his or her concerns seriously.

Should you agree with everything the buyer says? No. Do not humour buyers. This is an insult. Listen to criticisms carefully. A buyer may have a legitimate complaint. Acknowledge it. For example, you've given a tour of the house. The potential buyers have taken their time and gone through the house a second time on their own. You ask them what they think:

> Buyer: The house is nice, but the kitchen cupboards are too small for my antique china collection.
>
> You: Don't worry about it, Mrs. Jones. I'm sure they'll fit.

How can you be sure? Do you have the same type of china as Mrs. Jones? *Don't patronize the buyer*. Cupboard space is a practical consideration for many people. If Mrs. Jones has already visualized her valuable china in your cupboards, she's thinking seriously about buying your home. Don't ruin a sale by handling a buyer's concerns in a flippant manner.

Consider the following alternate response to the same situation:

> Buyer: The house is nice, but the kitchen cupboards are too small for my antique china collection.

> You: Let's take a closer look (open the cupboards). There are three rows of shelves that are eighteen inches wide, with an extra shelf above the stove. If that's not enough, the dining room has ample room for a buffet, which you can use to put them on display.

or

> You: I agree with you. Antique china does require more storage space than regular dishes. You might have to install new cupboards that will better suit your unique requirements. However, I'm sure you'll agree that you won't have to change anything else in the house. If you would like to make an offer, I'm sure we can negotiate.

Accept valid criticisms, but try to counter the impact by using some other attractive feature in your home as compensation. You have an interested buyer, otherwise he or she wouldn't bother to ask detailed questions. No home is perfect. A buyer doesn't expect perfection, but is entitled to satisfaction.

Be a Good Listener

Pay close attention to what buyers say about your home. No one likes to repeat himself; least of all, strangers who are considering an investment as large as a new home. Being a good listener is both courteous and professional. It also pays off. Put yourself in the buyer's position. From whom would you rather buy a house? Someone who won't let you get a word in edgewise, or ignores whatever you say, or interrupts? Or someone who makes eye contact, and thoughtfully responds to a question?

Listening is an art. It requires the ability to forget about yourself and your house, and give 100% concentration to the buyer. After all, you aren't trying to sell the house to yourself, are you?

Have Confidence in Your Product

Does your home give you pleasure? At the end of the day, are you glad to get home and put your feet up? Do you enjoy listening to your stereo or lounging in front of the fireplace? do you like sitting in the backyard, grilling a steak on the barbeque? Is your home a refuge—a friend to come home to after a day of work? Can you bring to mind pleasant memories of time spent in your house? Simply put, do you love your home?

If the answer is yes, you'll be able to sell it without difficulty. A good salesman believes in his product.

Any real-estate agent can find out that your house is a twelve-year-old stucco backsplit with gas heating. This is not what will sell it. *The comforts are what will ultimately sell your home.*

Corny as it may sound, for many buyers, a home is a lifestyle. It's a dream come true for first homeowners. During the 1950s, the young bride would dream of owning "a house with a white picket fence." Things haven't changed too much. For retired couples, a home is security, privacy, convenience and peace. For sophisticated, upwardly-mobile types, a home is status and a personal statement.

Seasoned buyers know what they're looking for in a home. They want to find it and feel it in yours. When buyers look through your home, they are trying to picture themselves living in it, just as you did when you first bought the house.

Being a homeowner gives you credibility in selling. A real-estate agent can comment to buyers about your "lovely" kitchen, but that's all. You're the one who has cooked, cleaned, canned vegetables, eaten and played cards in that room for years. You know its strong and weak points, because you have *experienced* them.

Convey an Interest in the Product

You have to make your product appeal to buyers. As long as you don't overprice yourself, this should be simple.

Think of a buyer's decision to purchase your home as being composed of three parts; physical, emotional and intcllcctual.

To appeal to the physical aspect of the decision-making process, ensure all repairs to the house have been completed (handrails, doors, and windows are in working order), and the furnace, plumbing and wiring are all intact. Buyers want to be sure basic physical requirements will be met. A couple of examples; they don't have to worry about being cold in the winter, due to poor heating or inadequate insulation; and there's lots of hot water for showering and cooking, because the plumbing and hot water heater are in order.

Create an atmosphere or a mood in your home to appeal to the emotional aspect of buying a home. Emotionally, buyers know they'll feel good when they curl up with a glass of wine in front of the fireplace, and can relax in the backyard. They'll enjoy their morning coffee while looking at the view through the bright kitchen window.

To appeal to the intellect, you must ask a reasonable price for the house. Buyers will calculate the projected worth of the home years down the road, when they sell. Intellectually, they know it's a good location and will be easy to resell.

They won't buy unless all three needs have been met and are in harmony. If you're not convinced that satisfying emotional, physical and intellectual needs are important factors in the decision to buy your home, take a closer look at the newspaper ads. The ads promise a great deal more than a brick building with plumbing and wiring. Consider phrases like:

> "tranquility space,"
> "horse lovers haven,"
> "lawn mower bye! bye! and away with your shovel when you move into this gorgeous townhouse,"
> "one of a kind. The mark of success. A truly distinguished home . . . A rare find,"
> "a touch of country,"
> "cozy living with fireplace,"
> "'mechanics special' Here is your chance to be self-employed at home!"
> "say goodbye to apartment life and hello to a home of your own,"
> "hassle-free living,"
> "old charm—new comforts,"
> "pick your own strawberries,"
> "antique lovers . . . will appreciate this early 1900s home,"
> "impress your friends . . . with this prestigious address,"
> "live free. Excellent opportunity to own a stately home and let the tenants pay your mortgage."

These are all examples of real ads.

You don't need a diploma to sell your house. You don't need to use ten-dollar words or technical jargon. Don't alienate potential buyers. Embrace them.

Use clear, simple language. Appeal to buyers' wants and needs. Quietly mention how much you've enjoyed barbequing in the backyard . . . how you're going to miss sitting in front of the fireplace, once the cold weather sets in. Make your building feel like home, and make it easy to buy it now.

CHAPTER 10

PROTECTING YOUR INTEREST

CAN A BUYER AFFORD YOUR HOUSE?

You have a serious buyer. He wants to put an offer in writing. Can he afford your home?

Real-estate agents will tell you they screen potential buyers before showing them your house. This is to save you the agonizing disappointment of having a deal fall through, because of a buyer's inability to acquire financing.

The real-estate agent will ask the potential buyers several questions related to employment, maximum amount they could afford for a down payment, and so on. This is not a foolproof system. An uncommitted buyer is under no legal obligation to reveal outstanding debts or bills to the real-estate agent.

It's difficult to tell, from the moment someone walks into your house, if they afford to buy it. Relying upon annual gross income as the sole criterion does not provide an absolute guarantee that a buyer can afford your home. Regardless of how high their earnings are some people always live beyond their means. Alternatively, someone who does not earn an outstanding income may have carefully saved for a number of years, and is in a position to put a 25% down payment on your house.

Unless you plan to trade your house for a Rolls Royce, it can be bought in only two ways—clear cash or financed cash (mortgage). The majority of buyers will be in the latter category. Ultimately, the mortgagee (buyer's bank or mortgage company) will determine whether the buyer can afford your home.

Arranging financing is the buyer's responsibility—not yours. Still, it would be helpful to know in advance if someone can afford your property.

FACTORS THAT DETERMINE WHETHER THE BUYER CAN AFFORD YOUR HOME

Since you've already gone through the process of buying at least one home, you are obviously familiar with the factors involved in determining whether or not a buyer can afford your house. In case you've forgotten, here are a few basic rules of thumb to refresh your memory.

Total Price of a Home Should not Be More Than 3.5 Times the Buyer's Annual Net Income

If you're prepared to ask the buyer his *net* income (and the buyer is prepared to tell you), the total price of the home and property should not exceed 3.5 times his or her net income. In other words, if the buyer's *net* annual income is $30,000, he or she cannot afford a home worth more than $105,000. Some working couples will buy a house together. The mortgagee will consider their joint income, in determining if they can afford your house.

As you're well aware, it costs money to maintain a house. This factor is taken into account when deciding if a buyer can afford your home. A second rule that applies in this estimate is:

Mortgage Payments (Principal and Interest) and Taxes Should not Exceed 25% to 30% of a Buyer's Gross Monthly Income.

Again, if you are prepared to ask the buyer his gross monthly income (and the buyer agrees to divulge this information), you can calculate whether the buyer can afford your home. If a buyer's *gross* monthly income is $1200, and your mortgage, interest and taxes total $800 per month, it's impossible for this buyer to maintain your home. The minimum monthly gross income required to pay monthly expenses of $800 is $2100.

Thus, if your rapport with your buyer is such that you can obtain reliable information about his or her gross monthly income and net annual income, you can easily calculate whether or not the buyer can afford your home. (This is assuming the buyer does not have other outstanding expenses or monthly payments.)

I chose not to discuss potential buyers' incomes or financial status. Prior to signing an Offer To Purchase, a buyer can easily change his or her mind. This stage of selling the house is fragile, and I was not willing to risk insulting, and thus losing, a buyer.

I got burned twice. What happened?

My first buyer was also the first person who looked at my home. He told me how much he loved the house and described all the changes he was going to make. He fully intended to buy the house, and not to worry, he could afford it.

Guess what? He couldn't afford it. When the time came to seriously negotiate, he was nowhere to be found. A week later, I found out (from another source) that he had approached the bank for pre-approved mortgage financing, and could not get the loan. He was recently divorced and heavily in debt.

In the interim, I wasted valuable time. Rather than keep my house on the market, I fretted over what had happened. What had I done wrong? This buyer wouldn't even return my calls.

The second time a deal fell through was devastating. An elderly woman and her sister wanted to buy my house. She had recently sold her own home and had only a few weeks to find another place. The pair planned to move in together and share expenses. Since she had just sold her home, I assumed (incorrectly, as I was soon to find out) she could afford to buy mine.

This buyer made an offer on the house before she had even seen the backyard. It was an *excellent* offer. However, she wasn't sure if she wanted my Jacuzzi included as part of the deal. The next day I called her (she had readily agreed to provide her name and phone number) and she definitely wanted to buy the house, Jacuzzi and all. Her sister had talked her into buying the Jacuzzi. (This is what I mean by letting the family do the rest of the selling for you.) I wasted no time in calling my lawyer. He was kind enough to agree to an appointment the next day (Saturday). We signed the Offer to Purchase and shook hands on the deal. I was in ecstasy and celebrated for the rest of the weekend.

My joy was short-lived. Two days later, the bottom fell out. I arrived home to find my buyer on my doorstep, in tears because she was denied financing from the bank. She couldn't get a mortgage. I was in total disbelief.

I spent most of the next day looking into the matter. My buyer was on a fixed income. Although she had made a profit selling her home, there was still a large outstanding balance to pay on the mortgage. Neither her bank nor any other bank or mortgage company in town would seriously consider the fact that she intended to share house expenses with her sister, who was also on a fixed income. What if personal difficulties arose and the two split up, leaving one alone to bear the burden of paying all the bills? My buyer needed a cosigner on the loan. She had no one who was willing to cosign on her behalf.

I considered taking out a second mortgage. Repeatedly I was advised against this plan. Given the circumstances, I would be better off to let the deal go and to put my house up for sale again. The deal fell through.

My disappointment with this turn of events cut me right to the bone. I liked the buyer and felt she would be happy living in my home. I was discouraged and didn't feel up to putting the house back on the market. Later, I began to feel angry. What right did this buyer have to lead me to believe she could afford my house? She wasted my time.

This buyer's mistakes were made in good faith. Some people are not good with finances, and honestly don't know if they can afford your home. They leave this up to the bank to sort out. The buyer had not deliberately tried to deceive me.

I don't believe a real-estate agent could have prevented this disaster. While discussing the matter with my bank manager, she pointed out that this type of thing also happens to competent real-estate agents. No method of screening buyers is infallible.

The lesson? "Buyer beware" is a popular expression. However, when you're in the business of selling your home, you must also protect yourself. Without being distrustful of buyers, there is a need to protect yourself against the onslaught of potential financial problems.

A deal is not a deal until the money is in your hands. Anything can, and does, happen in the interim. Keep your home on the market. If a second buyer does come along while you're waiting to see if the first buyer can get mortgage approval, simply advise the second buyer of this fact. You are not in a position to sell your home again, until the time given to the first buyer to obtain financing has lapsed (written in the Offer To Purchase). However, you can ask for the second buyer's name and phone number. In the event that the first deal falls through, you have a back-up buyer.

The second lesson? Don't give up. Real-estate agents do not have a perfect method of screening buyers. If you do give up, there's no guarantee that a real-estate agent will not run into the same problem with a new buyer.

CHAPTER 11

THE ART OF NEGOTIATION

Successfully negotiating the sale of your home is like playing a good card hand.

Don't plan on getting rich, but don't settle for breaking even. Know your rock-bottom price, but always ask for more, initially. This leaves room for negotiating the final price.

DON'T GET BOGGED DOWN IN DETAIL—FIRST GET AN OFFER

Sometimes buyers would look through my house, and ask if household items (such as the drapes or fridge and stove) were being included in the deal. I always gave the same answer:

"I'd like to include the drapes, because I think they belong with the house, and it would be a shame not to leave them. I would certainly entertain the possibility of making some kind of arrangement for the fridge and stove. If you're interested, why not make an offer and we can discuss it further?"

Don't let anyone trap you into making promises before you've even gotten an offer. If you don't mind selling household items in addition to the house, there's no harm in telling the buyer. However, there is a real danger in getting overinvolved in details too soon.

Never forget that your objective is to sell the house. You are not having a garage sale. When the subject of including or selling household items comes up, gently bring the buyer back to the main subject—the house. Afterwards, there'll be plenty of time to discuss the ancillary details.

THE OFFER

Unless buyers are naive, they will always offer you less than your asking price. This is to be expected. Buyers are testing the water to see how low you'll drop the price of your home. Business requires the use of negotiation to come to a satisfactory conclusion for both parties.

To negotiate successfully, you must know your rock-bottom price. Use this as your guideline for determining if an offer is worth consideration. (Keep this figure to yourself.)

Be prepared for some real lulus. My asking price was $51,900. My rock-bottom price was $48,500. One buyer kept hounding me to give my rock-bottom price. I repeated my asking price and suggested that he make an offer. This went on for about five minutes. He then made an offer of $35,000. I laughed. This buyer assured me that he could build a new house at that price. I counted to three and said, "I wish you all the luck in the world. You're certainly going to need it if you think you can build a new house for that price."

I showed this couple to the door. Insults do not need to be seriously addressed. I wasn't rude, but the conversation was over.

The next evening, while I was showing the house to someone else, I received a telephone call inquiring about the monthly operating costs of my Jacuzzi. I recognized the voice as belonging to the spouse from the previous night. I said, "I'm sorry. Your husband made an insulting offer on my house, and I don't care to give out any further information." She apologized for her husband's behaviour, and said he had insulted my home out of ignorance.

There's a point of no return. Even if he had improved his offer, I would not have sold him my house. A slap in the face is a slap in the face.

This works both ways. Suppose you've overpriced your home. Be prepared for the consequences, if you turn down a fair, realistic offer. Later on, when you don't get better offers, you'll realize that you've set your price too high. You'll approach the buyer who made the first offer, and tell him that you have reconsidered, and now wish to accept the offer. This buyer may no longer be interested. You've insulted his fair offer. Even if you decide to further drop the price, it may be too late. The buyer has reached his point of no return, thanks to your blundering greed.

FOR SALE BY OWNER

Most buyers will point out that you're saving a substantial real-estate commission, and will pressure you to drop your price accordingly.

This is fair game. However, you may have already taken this factor into account in your asking price. Let buyers know about this. Ask them to make an offer.

Don't start dropping your asking price before the buyer makes an offer. This is not how to successfully play the game. The buyer is fishing for your lowest price before he or she will commit to an offer. You've taken the first step by stating an asking price. The buyer knows what it is. The next step is up to the buyer. He or she must decide whether or not to make an offer, based on your asking price.

COUNTER-DISCUSS, INSTEAD OF ARGUING

The buyer is interested. You know he wants to make an offer:

> Buyer: I like your house. I saw one like it last week at 123 Main Street, that had a finished basement. He was asking only $148,000, not $151,900.
>
> You: That's right. But mine has a fireplace, and is in a better location.
>
> Buyer: $4000 is a lot to ask for a fireplace.
>
> You: That's not all. My house is available for immediate occupancy. You're looking to move in right away. That other house won't be ready for three months. Think of what you'll save if you buy my house.
>
> Buyer: Well . . . I don't know.
>
> You: Why not make an offer? Tell me what you would be willing to pay for the house, and I'll think it over.

You haven't argued with the buyer. You've acknowledged his legitimate comments, but have *countered* with other information. This is negotiating. By indirectly stating that your asking price is flexible, you have left the door wide open for the buyer to make an offer.

MAINTAIN A BARGAINING POSITION FOR AS LONG AS POSSIBLE

A buyer asks, "Your ad says you are asking $151,900. What's the lowest price you'll accept?" How do you respond?

Repeat your asking price and ask the buyer to make an offer. Under no circumstances reveal your rock-bottom price. Once you do, the game is over. No one would be willing to pay more for your house than is absolutely necessary. Stating the lowest price is the same as considering it sold at that price (or worse yet, even lower).

Maintain a bargaining position for as long as possible. Once you've named a price, there's no turning back. You can no longer ask one cent more for the house. Selling a house is serious business. Take your time before answering questions. You can't say, "Oh darn, I meant to ask $149,900, not $148,900." A serious buyer will think you're an amateur and will likely forget the whole idea of buying your house.

What if a buyer makes you an offer that's within range, but isn't quite as high as you had hoped it would be? Take your time. Tell the buyer you want to think about the offer for a day or so. This is permissible. Buying a home is a big decision. Deciding on the final selling price is also a major decision. Giving yourself one or two days to think about an offer maintains your bargaining position. Remember, if you accept an offer on the spot, the house is as good as sold for that price. When it comes time to put the offer in writing, you can't ask for more money without losing your credibility (and probably a sale).

SPLITTING THE DIFFERENCE

You're in a quandry. Your asking price is $153,800. A buyer offers you $150,000. What do you do?

An offer of $150,000 is not unreasonable. Your rock-bottom price is $148,500. You expected to come down from your initial asking price. Most buyers also expect to pay a slightly higher figure than their offer. That is, unless they say it's a *firm* offer, meaning it is not negotiable.

Both buyer and seller want to save face. If you want more than $150,000, justify the extra amount in a manner that will be acceptable to the buyer.

One option is to split the difference. You can use a portion of your savings on the real-estate commission, and still make a profit. For example:

> Seller: I've had time to think about your offer of $150,000. It's not a bad offer, but you're asking me to drop my price by almost $4,000. How about if we split the difference, say an even $2,000. Increase your offer to $152,000 and we'll call it a deal?
>
> Buyer: The most I can spent is $151,000.
>
> Seller: OK, you've got a deal.

You've stated an option that was acceptable to the buyer. He didn't meet your quite halfway, but did significantly increase his original offer. Some sellers would continue to haggle until they got an additional few dollars, but this is an individual decision. Personally, I don't agree with haggling for the sake of a few hundred dollars. After all, you're selling a house worth many thousands of dollars, not a second-hand motorcycle. You've done a good deal. Be satisfied.

SWEETEN THE DEAL WITHOUT SELLING FOR LESS

Suppose offering to split the difference doesn't work. The buyer can't afford to spend more money than he's already offered. If you want to improve on an offer, consider the following alternatives:

Alter the Possession Date

A flexible possession date can be your ace in the hole. Consider your buyer's position. If he or she is stuck in an unsatisfactory apartment, an early possession date will be highly desirable. If you can make your home available for immediate occupancy, tell buyers of the rent saving for the next two or three months. (Particularly, if they have to pay additional costs for hydro and utilities.) If they buy your house now, they'll be *saving* money.

Consider the position of a buyer who has already sold his home and is living with friends or relatives, or in a motel. This person is champing at the bit to move into a house. Immediate possession will give this person peace of mind.

The opposite situation occurs when a buyer has put in an offer on your home, but still has to sell his own home. This buyer could greatly benefit from a later possession date. Who wants to pay to maintain two houses at the same time? Delaying the possession date, without lowering your asking price, will save this buyer a *substantial* amount of money. However, you must carefully consider this option before suggesting it. After all, unless there's some benefit to keeping your home an additional two or three months, you're still responsible for maintaining the house (and probably paying a mortgage). This additional cost will lessen the total profit. If there's no purpose in continuing to own your house, you might be better off to sell immediately, for less money.

Include Household Items as Part of the Sale

Another way to sweeten the deal without lowering your price is by including household items in the sale. Choose articles that not only will appeal to the buyer, but that you will not need to replace. For example;

Buyer: All I can afford to offer at this time is $150,000.

Seller: I've already dropped my price by $3,000 to $151,000. However, I'd like to throw in some things with the house that I know you'll need (all the drapes, lawnmower, garden equipment, pool chemicals and so on).

Buyer: OK, it's a deal.

This technique often works. The buyer is getting something tangible to balance the increase in cost. It didn't cost you any money, and both parties feel satisfied.

DON'T NICKEL AND DIME

You can't afford to lose the sale of your house by haggling over petty details. Suppose a buyer has made you a fair offer, but also wants to buy your stove for a song. You know you're being underpriced for the stove, but so what? If you stand to gain a substantial profit from the sale of your house, is it really worth it to argue about the price of a second-hand stove? If the sale goes through, you can afford to be generous. Why not make the buyer feel good and give him the stove?

The same rationale holds for other household items. Along with the house, many buyers want to have the drapes, or the rugs. What can you do with the drapes in your new house? Use these items either to sweeten the deal, or as your ace in the hole for clinching the deal. For example:

> Buyer: You have a nice house. The price is fair, but I don't know. I guess we can't make up our minds.
>
> Seller: I don't want to pressure you, but it is a good deal.
>
> Buyer: We don't have any major appliances and would have to buy a fridge and stove.
>
> Seller: Tell you what. If you really want the house, I'll throw my fridge and stove in as part of the deal.
>
> Buyer: That sounds fair. OK, we'll buy it.

MAKE THE BUYER FEEL HE HAS MADE A BARGAIN

A house is a major purchase. Buyers are bound to have second thoughts about their decision. Once a deal is made, you don't want anything to go wrong. You don't want a buyer to change his or her mind at the last minute. It's important to help a buyer feel he or she has done well by purchasing your home. This is another reason it doesn't hurt to include a few extras in the deal. It won't cost you much, but it will leave your buyer satisfied and content with the purchase.

CHAPTER 12

THE PITFALLS OF OVERPRICING

It's human nature to want the best price possible for your home. Suppose an appraiser estimates the value of your house to be $114,000. There's no legal obligation to use this exact figure as the price for which you sell your home. For some homeowners, there's a real temptation to tack on extra dollars to the asking price. Most people own only a few homes in their lifetimes, so you won't get many chances to make this type of "easy money." Right? All you need is one naive buyer who's willing to pay an inflated amount, because he or she can't live without your house. After all, if no one's interested in buying at your first price, you can always drop your price later. Right?

Examine your reasons for selling your own home. Are you interested in saving yourself a 6% real-estate commission? As I mentioned earlier, for practical reasons, most real-estate agents have to sell your home for less than its actual appraised value. If your home is worth $150,000, most agents will ask you to list for $148,000, because it's much easier to sell at that price. The extra $120 commission for selling at the higher price is not cost-effective for the real-estate agent, who has to sell several homes simultaneously to stay in business. You, on the other hand, stand to gain $2,000, plus the $9,000 savings for selling it on your own. This extra $11,000 is based on selling your home for its actual value. Don't forget, if you list your home at $148,000, you'll sell for less, probably $147,000 at the most, or as low as $145,500. By selling on your own, you could save thousands of tax-free dollars, while still selling the house for its appraised value.

Selling your own home should result in a fair profit. Don't plan on getting rich. You'll waste a great deal of valuable time—and you still won't get rich.

If there is one absolute truth in real estate it's this: *The higher the house is priced, the more work it is to sell.*

Most buyers aren't naive. They can't afford that luxury. Your house is in competition with others on the market. If your asking price is not in the same range as similar homes, most buyers will realize it. Very few people buy the first home they see, without shopping around for a deal. Asking price should be based on realistic, rather than emotional, factors. Even though you might be emotionally attached to your house (which is reflected in your price), a buyer is not.

I CAN ALWAYS DROP MY PRICE LATER

This is not as simple as it might seem. First of all, you must attract buyers through advertising. Put yourself in the buyer's position. You're looking through the newspaper ads and find several houses within your price range. You see another ad that describes a house you might like, but the asking price is significantly higher than the other homes. Which ones are you going to consider? Are you going to waste time following up the last ad, thinking the seller will eventually come down to a realistic price?

By asking an exorbitant price, you'll eliminate many potential buyers from the outset. This is a serious mistake. Selling on your own is more difficult than hiring a real-estate agent. Real-estate companies have a greater pool of buyers. You have to maximize your advertising efforts, in order to attract potential buyers. An unrealistically high price destroys buyer interest.

Most buyers have a price range in mind. Psychologically and financially, they may not be prepared to pay more than a fixed amount. Buying ceilings are important. Buyers looking for something in the $80,000 price range will glean through ads that describe houses up to and including that amount.

Let's suppose your home is within this range. Your rock bottom price is $77,500. Even though you eventually hope to get $79,500 or $80,000 for your home, you advertise for an additional $5000.00. Your asking price is $84,500, which is the amount you quote in the newspaper.

What risks are involved with using this approach? By advertising a house worth $79,000 for $84,500, you will have crossed a psychological barrier for most appropriate buyers. They won't bother to respond to your ad, because they can't afford your asking price, *even though they could afford your final price*.

Real-estate agents use psychology in price setting. $79,900 sounds better than $80,000, $84,900 sounds better than $85,000, and so on. Although, financially, $100 doesn't make a significant difference in the price of a house, such a technique serves the purpose of avoiding a psychological barrier.

You might be thinking, "But if I want $79,000 and I advertise for $79,000, I won't have any room for bargaining later on."

By advertising an asking price very close to the realistic amount you expect to obtain for your house (say $79,000), you'll have more buyers coming over to consider your house; therefore more chances to get $79,000. One option is to state in your ad; "$79,000 *firm*." This means there is no room to negotiate the asking price. However, if buyers respond to this ad, they are not likely to haggle, if the asking price is fair.

Suppose you've decided to go ahead and advertise for $84,500. After a few unsuccessful weeks, you decide to drop the price to a more realistic figure of $82,500. This is bound to attract some interest, particularly in buyers (and real-estate agents) who regularly read the house ads. Unless you have a completely different description of your house to accompany the lower asking price, most buyers will recognize your ad.

Without realizing it, you may have started a buyer cat-and-mouse game. Consider the buyer reading your ad:

> Mary: Look John, here's that same house near the high school. They've dropped their price by $2,000.
>
> John: Oh, that's good. It's still too expensive.
>
> Mary: Let's wait another couple of weeks and see if they drop the price again.

This happens all the time. You are now advertising that your home is not worth your original asking price. Buyers want a bargain, and will wait you out.

Don't be surprised if you start getting calls from real-estate agents. They also read the newspaper ads, and will be the first to spot your change in price. They'll volunteer their services, because obviously you're having problems selling on your own. And you are. But only because you're asking for too much money, not because the house is difficult to sell.

PRICING YOURSELF OUT OF THE MARKET

No one wants something if no one else wants it. A house is much easier to sell while it's in demand. Buyers are leery of homes that don't sell quickly. There must be something wrong with it, if it isn't sold by now.

Homes that don't sell soon get a bad reputation. Buyers know it and so do real-estate agents. Even if you do drop your price, you may have already lost a large percentage of buyers. They no longer trust your property, because it's been for sale too long.

Selling houses is a competitive business. You have to pit your house against the rest on the market. It would be a shame to lose out because you overpriced yourself.

YOU MAY END UP LOSING MONEY

You may believe that, by advertising at an unrealistic price, you will at least end up with a fair price. It doesn't often work this way.

Eventually, you'll have to lower your price to a reasonable figure, and the best you can expect is to sell the house for what it's worth. If it's left on the market too long, you'll probably end up selling for less than if you had originally asked for a fair price.

Time is money. The longer it takes to sell your house, the more money it costs. Think about it. If it takes four months, instead of one, to sell your house, this represents an additional three months of expenses to maintain the house—mortgage, interest, heat, hydro, utilities and so on. You must subtract these additional costs from the selling price to arrive at your profit figure. Is it worth it? Have you saved money or lost money in the long run?

If you don't sell within a reasonable time, you may find yourself in the unfortunate position of adding unnecessary complications to your life. What if you have to start a new job in another location? You might have to buy a second home, without having sold the first. Maintaining two houses at the same time can be difficult, if not financially draining.

A GOOD DEAL IS NOT ALWAYS MEASURED IN DOLLARS AND CENTS

Successfully selling your own house doesn't always mean making a fortune. A good deal for you might be the luxury of setting your own possession date. For reasons of your own, you might want to live in your house for a few more months. Although you might have to sell for a lesser amount of money, you've gained in the long run, because your needs have been met and you have peace of mind.

Alternatively, you might have seen your dream house, and want to sell your own house immediately. Although you might have to sell for less, you are now in a position to buy that fantastically-priced second house. It doesn't show up on paper, but you've made a profit.

Thus, not all good deals are measured in dollars and cents.

Sell your house and get on with your life. Don't plan on getting rich. You won't. That isn't the idea. Don't let greed turn a potentially rewarding experience into your worst nightmare.

CHAPTER 13

BEGINNER'S LUCK

SHOULD YOU SELL TO THE FIRST BUYER?

Your ad has been in the newspaper for an hour and someone calls to see the house. He looks the place over, and gives you a good offer.

Although rare, this situation does occur. Beginner's luck has struck again. What should you do? Should you hold out for a better offer? After all, you've already paid in advance to keep your ad in the paper for another two days. You're all psyched up for selling, and haven't had much of a chance.

My advice? SELL, SELL, SELL. You have achieved the goal of selling your home. Don't hold out, because you think you might get a better offer if you wait. Your next offer might be a long time in coming and, when you finally do get another offer, it might be lower than your first. In the meantime, the first buyer will no longer be available.

Perhaps you're plagued by the possibility that you've underpriced your house. This would account for it being so painlessly easy to sell. This is unlikely, if you've set your asking price within range of market analyses or formal appraisal values.

Sell the house now. Keep in mind that, the longer it takes to sell your house, the more it costs—additional maintenance, mortgage and interest payments, heat, hydro, utilities and so on—to say nothing of the emotionally draining experience of waiting for the "right" buyer.

If you still can't decide, read Chapter 15 (House Selling Blues). That should convince you to go ahead and SELL. However, before you crack open the champagne, *please keep your house on the market*. A deal isn't closed until the money is in your possession.

CHAPTER 14

WHY DEALS FALL THROUGH

FINANCING

The most common reason for a deal falling through is the buyer's inability to obtain adequate financing. He or she cannot obtain a mortgage or loan to pay for your house.

Most Offers To Purchase contain a clause that makes the sale of the house conditional upon the buyer's ability to secure financing within a set period of time. In other words, if the buyer can't get a mortgage, the deal is off. The full deposit is returned to the buyer. You end up with nothing but lost time.

What can you do to prevent this? To ensure that time is not wasted showing the home to buyers who are unable to afford the price, most real-estate agents promise to screen buyers. Often, they do have an advantage, because they either know the buyers, or are aware of buyers who habitually look for homes beyond their means. However, as mentioned earlier, no one has perfected a method of ensuring that only financially secure individuals will buy your home.

By asking the buyer her gross monthly income and annual net income, you can determine quite accurately whether or not the buyer can afford your home. This is assuming the buyer truthfully reveals this information, and has no other outstanding debts.

Ultimately, the mortgagee investigates to determine if the buyer can afford your home. All the buyer's cards are on the table, and if he can't afford the house, it becomes painfully obvious to all concerned.

What to do? By far, the most important step is to keep your house on the market while you're waiting to see if a deal goes through. NEVER, NEVER, NEVER LOSE VALUABLE SELLING TIME. It's difficult to regain the selling momentum, if you prematurely remove your house from the market. It's hard to psych yourself up again and again.

NEGOTIATE FOR THE OPTIMAL FINANCING PERIOD

Once you sign an Offer To Purchase, you are not legally free to sell to a new buyer until the time allotted to the first buyer to obtain financing has lapsed. This date is clearly stated in the Offer to Purchase. Shortly after signing the Offer To Purchase, it may become obvious that the buyer will never be able to obtaining financing. However, you're still legally bound to honour the date set in the contract, before selling to someone else.

The period of time that a buyer has to obtain financing is a *negotiable* feature of the Offer To Purchase. It's in your best interests to arrange the shortest possible time, in order to prevent your home from being locked in for an extended period.

However, you must give the buyer a fair chance to obtain a mortgage. Most buyers plan on putting a 10% down payment on your house. Before granting mortgage approval, a mortgagee will routinely require that your home be appraised. Arrangements for the appraisal take at least two or three days. If the buyer is putting a larger down payment on your house (usually 25%), appraisals are not routinely ordered.

A standard period of time for allowing the buyer to obtain financing is seven to ten working days. In other words, to protect yourself should a deal fall through, don't tie up your home for longer than two weeks.

There may be extenuating circumstances. For example, a buyer may want your home, but has to sell his own before he is in a position to buy yours. This is a difficult situation. If you opt to accept a written offer from this buyer, how long should you wait to see if the buyer can sell his own home? I would discuss this matter carefully with either your lawyer or bank manager. If the buyer can't sell his own home in time, you have the most to lose.

ADVANCE MORTGAGE APPROVAL

Most banks and mortgage institutions offer a service called *advance mortgage approval*. Prior to signing an Offer To Purchase, a buyer approaches a bank with information about the cost of the home. The mortgagee will review the buyer's income, monthly expenses, outstanding loans and debts. Based on these criteria, the potential homebuyer will be told the amount of money the mortgagee is willing to loan, or will be granted advance mortgage approval to this set figure.

To a seller, this service is a lifesaver. You know ahead of time whether or not a buyer can afford your home. You have peace of mind that a deal will not fall through because of financing problems. Prior to putting an offer in writing, I highly recommend that you suggest this service (provided free of charge) to an interested buyer.

HOUSE IS OVERPRICED

This is another reason why deals fall through. As previously mentioned, many buyers put a 10% down payment on a house. Before granting mortgage approval, the mortgagee routinely orders a professional appraisal of your home. Suppose you're selling your house for $83,000, but the appraisal comes in "light" at the lower price of $80,000. The mortgagee will give a loan based only on the appraised value of $80,000, not $83,000. The most they will loan is 90% of the appraised value or, in this case, 90% of $80,000 or $72,000.

If the buyer decides to go through with the deal, he or she has to come up with the $2,700 difference in cash, in addition to the 10% ($8,300) downpayment. In other words, the buyer has to make a 13.2% downpayment, or give you $11,000 cash, not 10% or $8,300.

This puts a different perspective on the sale of your house. In fact, *most Offers to Purchase are conditional upon the appraised value of the house matching or exceeding the sale price*. So, if you've overpriced your home, (according to the professional appraiser hired by the bank), the buyer can legally back out of the deal.

If you think you're asking a fair price for the house, you can always register a complaint. That is, you can take the appraiser to court and sue for the difference. Professional appraisers are usually chartered, meaning that they are members of an association governed by a professional code, and are accountable for their actions.

You may not wish to get involved with expensive legal hassles at this time. However, like everyone else, appraisers are only human, and do make mistakes. If you're right, defend your rights.

BUYER GETS COLD FEET

A third reason for deals falling through is buyers changing their minds. This is unusual, but it does happen.

To prevent this from happening routinely, it's customary for the buyer to give a deposit at the time the Offer To Purchase is signed. Although this is not a law, it represents an act of good faith on the buyer's part. By giving a deposit, the buyer is saying he's serious about his intention to buy your home. If the buyer backs out of the deal for reasons that are not conditional within the Offer To Purchase, he will forfeit the deposit. In other words, if a buyer changes his mind about your house, you're entitled to the entire deposit as compensation for your wasted time.

In the case of a real-estate agent selling the home on behalf of a homeowner, he or she holds the deposit while the buyer is making financial arrangements. If you're selling the house on your own, its customary for your lawyer to hold the deposit.

Some books will give advice on how to write up your own Offer To Purchase. Although there is no legal requirement, I highly recommend hiring a lawyer to help both you and the buyer with the contractual arrangements of the Offer To Purchase. Although an Offer To Purchase is not difficult to draft, it must be precise (exact dates, and so on), otherwise it's a meaningless document (see Chapter 16 for details).

Hiring a lawyer to take care of this matter is in the best interests of both buyer and seller. A lawyer is obligated to inform *both buyer and seller* of their rights and obligations. Enlisting a lawyer's help to draw up the Offer To Purchase ensures that everything is on the up and up.

Put yourself in the buyer's spot. Wouldn't you feel better handing over a $5,000 deposit to a lawyer instead of a homeowner? I know I would. The fee incurred in hiring a lawyer for this service is nominal, compared to the peace of mind it provides for both buyer and seller.

CHAPTER 15

PLATEAUS AND OTHER LOWS

You're trying your best. The house looks great. The ad is good, and you're at home, patiently waiting. The first two weeks went reasonably well—lots of phone enquiries, a few buyers over to have a look. However, this week, the ad has been in the paper for four days and you've received only a few calls from superficially interested buyers. What are you doing wrong?

Unless you've overpriced the house, probably nothing. Plateaus happen to everyone, even the world's best real-estate agent. When this happened to me, I was concerned that I had overpriced the house, or my ad had been in the paper too long and I had exhausted the buyer population.

Two weeks later, business picked up. During an unrelated discussion with my lawyer, he mentioned that real-estate sales had been slow for everyone during that earlier period. In addition to a spell of intolerably hot weather, a new government budget was being proposed, which hinted at the possibility of taxing real-estate sales. Like other selling markets, real estate can be quite sensitive to a fluctuating political atmosphere.

The lesson: Don't give up easily. If real-estate agents know you're selling your own home, from time to time they'll try to discourage you. "If you had let me handle the sale, the house would probably have been sold by now, especially since I had two buyers who were very interested in a house just like yours."

Give yourself time. Two or three months is not an unreasonable period over which to sell your house. Need convincing? On your way to work, make a habit of noticing homes for sale by various real-estate companies. It's easy to spot these homes, because they have a big FOR SALE sign defacing the front yard. See how long it takes to sell them. Or, using the same methodical approach to reading stocks, follow different *For Sale* ads in the newspapers.

Not everyone gets a hole-in-one. Similarly, not everyone sells their home to the first buyer who walks in the front door.

DON'T COUNT YOUR CHICKENS . . .

A deal is not a deal until the money is in your pocket. I have previously described my experience of losing two deals on the sale of my house. I took for granted the ability of my buyers to obtain financing. In the interim, I stopped selling my house. This was a serious mistake. Once you've taken your home off the market, it's difficult to regain the enthusiasm and momentum required to sell it. Don't indulge yourself in a fool's paradise, thinking you've sold your home before all the details are complete. You may be unnecessarily setting yourself up for grievous disappointment.

WAFFLING OVER PRICE

In all likelihood, this won't happen to you. Before one of my deals fell apart, the buyer had made a fantastic offer, which barely put a dent in my asking price. The failure of this sale not only left me disappointed, it diminished my satisfaction with my previously set price.

I've stressed the importance of knowing both your asking price and rock-bottom price before selling your home. Prior to this "sale," I would have been satisfied with a considerably lower price. Since I had been offered the moon, stars and sun on paper, I had difficulty re-establishing my original set price, without feeling a sense of failure. Deep down, I knew I would never find another buyer who was willing to pay such an exorbitant amount for my house.

If a buyer doesn't have the money, it's easy to make an unrealistic offer on a house. My buyer couldn't back up her offer with cash and, therefore, had lost nothing in actually writing up the offer. I had lost time that would have been better spent showing the house to more appropriate buyers.

The lesson: Don't let bizarre circumstances interfere with a well-laid-out plan. Don't compound one error with another, by wavering from your original asking price (assuming it's fair). Stick by this amount, no matter what happens.

There is always a risk that someone who wants to buy your house will not be able to afford it. This doesn't mean you should alter your price or, worse yet, give up and let a real-estate agent take over. There are risks in any business venture. Roll with the punches and keep going.

LETTING TOO MUCH TIME ELAPSE BETWEEN SHOWINGS

Time passes quickly when you're selling your house. If you put the sale of your house on hold, while you're awaiting the outcome of a deal, you risk wasting valuable time. Remember, you have to give a buyer at least five to ten working days to obtain financing. If the deal falls through, you're behind by one or two weeks. This may not sound like much, but multiply this by a factor of two or three and it adds up to a considerable length of time.

Your objective is to sell your home and get on with your life. The longer it takes, the more money you lose, because you have to continue paying the costs of owning the house (mortgage, interest, hydro and so on).

I was inexperienced, and didn't want to deal with the possibility that I might have two interested buyers at the same time. I avoided this situation by taking my house off the market between serious offers. I would never do this again. You tend to put too much false hope into a deal, and end up disappointed and discouraged if things don't work out.

I suggest the following: if you have a serious offer, follow it up. In the interim, keep the house on the market. If another serious buyer appears, advise him or her of your situation. In the event the first deal is not successful, you'll have a back-up buyer. In this businesslike manner, you are protecting your interest, if the deal falls through.

Consider the strategies some real-estate agents use to sell houses. Some will bring two buyers to a house at the same time, to deliberately enhance the idea that the house is in demand. Others will pressure a buyer into putting in a written offer by saying that another couple is interested in the home, and wouldn't it be a shame to miss out on this deal by thinking about it for too long.

It's easier to sell a house that's still in demand. Don't compromise future sales by putting all your efforts into one written offer. Don't put all your eggs in one basket.

EVERYONE'S AN EXPERT

Most people have spent some time living in a house, even if they didn't own it themselves. Living in a house somehow bestows free licence for friends or family to comment on how you should get your home ready for show, what price to ask, and the like.

To a degree, such advice is harmless. However, if these opinions are tending to confuse rather than clarify issues, you have to intervene.

Be wary of comments that have a negative slant—"Don't bother to paint the bathroom, because the new owners will repaint it to suit their own taste." Undertake repairs or renovations necessary to enable you to feel confident about your ability to successfully show and sell the house.

Giving advice is easy, especially when you don't have anything to lose. However, it's a totally different matter when you're confronted by a stranger who is scrutinizing your home for the purposes of buying.

COPING WITH "HAVEN'T YOU SOLD THE HOUSE YET?"

To increase my free advertising, I told everyone I was selling my house. If you've followed this route, be prepared for the backlash. It doesn't matter if it has been only two weeks since you started selling your house. You may still be subjected to the incredulous "You haven't sold it yet?"

Laugh it off. Or better yet, say, "No, I haven't sold the house yet. Do you know someone who's interested?" Maximize your free advertising.

Whatever you do, don't tell friends you have a written offer. If the deal falls apart, you'll spare yourself the embarrassment of having to admit it. There's a time for celebration and a time for discretion. This is the time for discretion.

CLEANLINESS IS NEXT TO GODLINESS

A sure way to devalue your home is to have soiled carpeting, foul-smelling, messy bathrooms, chaotic closets, marks and fingerprints on light-switch panels and door handles, grimy sinks, and dust on your baseboards.

Selling your home may take up to two or three months. Unless you're obsessive-compulsive about cleanliness, keeping your home constantly immaculate can become tiring. After a month of selling my home, I told my mother I was thinking of staying over at friends so I wouldn't mess up my picture-perfect house. She told me it was time to sell the house and be done with it. "You still have to live in the house, you know."

If you reach the point where you don't want to leave a rinsed plate in the sink in case a buyer drops over, you might benefit from the following suggestions:

1. Postpone major messy or smelly jobs, like canning or furniture stripping, until you sell the house.

2. Keep one or two spare drawers. Use these for last-minute storage of scattered articles of clothing, magazines or other odds and ends. Remember, you have to keep the closets well organized *all the time*.

3. Have one showy bedspread on hand. If the sheets are wrinkled, no one will notice. Buyers will see only the attractive bedspread.

4. In an emergency, store items under beds. If the bedspreads reach the floor, no one will ever see what you've done. I have yet to see a buyer check under a bed.

GOOD IDEAS CAN BACKFIRE

Whenever a buyer was coming over to have a look at my house, I tried to add some finishing touch. My back yard was bordered by lilacs, so I filled the house with the sight and smell of these fresh-cut flowers. Lilacs were placed in the kitchen, bathrooms, bedroom and den.

Guess what happened? One buyer had a strong allergy to lilacs. He didn't buy my house. It hadn't occurred to me that one little extra touch might be my undoing. Instead of enhancing, it distracted from the overall mood I had created in the house.

Not everyone is allergic to lilacs. But don't overdo it; let the house sell itself.

SURPRISE VISITS FROM REAL-ESTATE AGENTS

As the old saying goes, "you don't get anything for free." If you've invited real-estate agents over to your home for the purpose of obtaining free market analyses, don't be surprised if some keep in touch with you, either by phone or by dropping over.

Real-estate agents know whether or not you have sold the house. By the time four to six weeks have passed, you might be discouraged and vulnerable to giving up. Lo and behold, the real-estate agents suddenly appears to help you out of your predicament.

Don't give up easily. Give yourself two or three months to sell the house. You've gotten this far, haven't you? At this stage, hiring a real-estate agent will give you no guarantee that he or she can find a buyer faster than you can on your own. If a house isn't selling, it's usually because the house is overpriced, not because of who is selling it.

HOMEBUYER'S EYE

> A woman puts a vase of fresh-cut, cheery flowers on her kitchen table. Suddenly she notices that the table looks drab. So she paints the table, which makes the walls look drab by comparison, so she paints the walls....

This woman has been afflicted with homebuyer's eye. She has learned to see her house as it is, complete with every glaring flaw.

One step ahead. Two steps back. Every improvement you make serves to magnify what's still left to do, generating yet more work.

For three weeks, this was an ongoing process in the preparation of my house. Until I cleaned up the eyesore that was my garden patch and driveway, I couldn't enjoy sitting on my backyard patio. Even minor projects gained momentum and became large projects. At first, I had intended to paint only one wall in my recreation room. However, by comparison the remaining walls looked dull, and I ended up painting the entire room.

If you're stuck with homebuyer's eye, there's only one cure. Fix up the house until you're satisfied. You won't regret it.

HOMESELLINGITIS

"Homesellingitis" is an advanced case of "homebuyer eye". This describes the mental set you may adopt, once the showing and selling business is seriously underway.

As time goes on, you may find that you're preoccupied with thoughts of selling your house. A totally unrelated conversation about the weather may remind you that you need to turn on the sprinklers so the grass looks green. An exchange of recipes may remind you that you forgot to hide that rusty toaster-oven sitting on the countertop for all to see.

Unlike homebuying eye, homesellingitis is not simple to cure. Although it's natural to temporarily adopt this type of thinking while you're selling your home, it does try the nerves of even your most patient friends. Particularly if your friends do not own a house, it can be difficult to accept the new you, who is always talking "house."

This behaviour can be compared with that of new parents, who now seem to be blind to all information other than that which they can relate to kids.

New parents often gravitate toward other new parents, so they can discuss similar interests *ad nauseam*, without feeling guilty or crazy. My saving grace was to find an acquaintance who had just sold his own home. It was great. I could discuss "house talk" at length without fear of being misunderstood, or boring other companions. This common interest rapidly developed into a close friendship. My friend could easily relate to my new frame of mind, and was helpful in encouraging me to try some ideas and suggesting even better ones.

I hope that, by the time this book is in print, homeowners who are selling on their own will be commonplace, and such soulmates will be easy to find. In the meantime, if you find yourself becoming preoccupied with the showing and selling process, let a friend "housesit" (stay at home to answer calls) for an evening or two. Go out for a walk. You'll soon feel rejuvenated and over your temporary "house fatigue." Selling a house is a big responsibility. Many thousands of dollars are at stake. People have allowed themselves to lose perspective over much less important issues. Take a break.

HOUSE AS INVESTMENT—NOT ALWAYS

I've always believed that owning a house was an old-fashioned, secure investment. Unless you bought a "bad" house, you were bound to make a profit when the time came to sell. This is not necessarily true.

According to Harris Mitchell (*Winnipeg Tribune*, April 19, 1979), buying a house is not always the best investment that you can make, because of market fluctuations. What if you buy at a time when houses are expensive, and then have to sell when the market is depressed, and houses have consequently depreciated in value?

According to Mitchell, buying a house may only be a good investment if you intend to keep the house for at least seven years, or the price of houses increased at an annual rate of 7% or more.

I sold my house after owning it for a short period of time (under three years), and the annual percentage increase for homes in my area was a mere 3%. It was a buyer's, not a seller's, market. To make matters worse, I had spent approximately $5,500 to renovate the house. To break even, I had to sell on my own.

Through hard work, I improved the appearance of my home to the point where I could ask top dollar. I asked a moderately higher selling price than my best "market analysis" figure, because time was on my side.

I realized a modest profit on the sale of my house. I didn't harbour any unrealistic dreams of getting rich, and therefore wasn't disappointed when this didn't happen. But I attained my goal of selling the house, with the least amount of pain.

Know your market. Know what to expect when you sell your house. Be realistic in price setting, and you won't go wrong. More important, you won't give up.

CHAPTER 16

THE LEGAL END

Arranging good legal assistance is an important aspect of selling on your own. Before you put an offer in writing, discuss your plans with a lawyer, and find one who can help you. Most are very willing to do so, and at a minimal cost.

A lawyer can replace a real estate agent

Even if you hire a real-estate agent, you still need to retain a lawyer to draft and register the Deed of Sale, discharge your mortgage, and attend to other legal matters related to the sale. However, many homeowners don't realize that a lawyer will also assume tasks normally undertaken by the real-estate agent, for a fraction of the cost.

THE OFFER TO PURCHASE

Consider the Offer to Purchase. Most of us expect the real-estate agent to complete and present the written offer to the buyer (before the buyer has a chance to change his mind). However, most lawyers are happy to draft up the Offer to Purchase within a period of time convenient to both you and your buyer.

Some books will give you advice on drafting your own Offer to Purchase and Deed of Sale documents. After all, if you're prepared to sell your own home, why shouldn't you prepare your own documents as well? Unless you possess expertise in drafting legal documents, this can be a highly risky endeavour.

BEWARE OF THE "STANDARD" FORM

Although you can find Offer to Purchase and Deed of Sale forms in most stationery stores, these may not be in an acceptable format for your area. Most provinces (and states) have their own forms, and a substitute may not be binding in a court of law. At the very least, using a nonstandard form creates needless confusion and extra work.

PRECISION DECISION

Writing up an offer is not complicated, but it does contain several parts, all of which must be meticulously worded and accurately completed. Otherwise, the contract may not be legally binding.

Take a close look at a completed Offer to Purchase (like the one you signed when you bought your house). The terms must be specific (for example; all curtains to be included except those in the master bedroom). Ambiguous words such as "necessary repairs" or "reasonable condition," used in the body of the Offer to Purchase, may invalidate the offer.

Mistakes can easily happen. For example, a mistake can occur if the buyer thinks he's getting the dishwasher as part of the agreement, but you had intended to sell it as a separate item. This misunderstanding may invalidate a written offer.

What about if you unknowingly misrepresent your property? You might believe the lilac bushes bordering the edge of your property line are yours, when they belong to your neighbour. This type of mistake, however innocent in intent, will invalidate a written offer.

The above are just a few examples of what can go wrong in writing up the Offer to Purchase. A competent lawyer can be of great help in drafting the documents clearly and accurately. After all your work, it would be a shame to create unnecessary problems and even botch a deal, because you wanted to save a few dollars (and I mean a *few* dollars).

ENSURE COMPREHENSION

Even more important than drafting the Offer to Purchase, a competent lawyer will help you (and your buyer) to *understand* the terms of the offer before you agree to sign it.

Your objective is to sell the house. If you sell your own home, you stand to save thousands of tax-free dollars. If you prepare your own legal documents, you will perhaps (at best) save a few hundred dollars. Financially, you have little to gain, and a great deal to lose, by relying on limited knowledge in drafting unfamiliar legal documents. It may even cost you the sale of your house.

SAFEGUARDING THE DEPOSIT

Although not a legal requirement, it's a customary show of good faith for a buyer to make a deposit after signing the Offer to Purchase. The deposit is your guarantee the buyer is making a serious commitment to purchase your home.

If the house is sold to the buyer, the deposit is used as partial payment of the house. Should the deal fall through, due to conditions not specified in the offer (for example, the buyer gets cold feet and changes his mind), the buyer forfeits the deposit to you.

Most of us expect a real-estate agent to obtain and secure the deposit until the deal is finalized. However, a lawyer will also perform this service.

Whatever you do, don't try to save yourself a few bucks and do this yourself. How many potential buyers do you think will hand a large sum of their hard-earned cash over to you? I wouldn't, and therefore did not place a potential buyer in this position.

All reasonable buyers appreciate the importance of the deposit. Because of their code of ethics, lawyers and real-estate agents seem the most reasonable people to hold the deposit while the deal is underway. Why not get the most from your money and leave this up to your lawyer?

USING A LAWYER INCREASES YOUR CREDIBILITY

Put yourself in the buyer's position. You're already going out on a societal limb, by selling your own home. In spite of this non-traditional approach, through hard work, you've found a potential buyer. Now, suppose you ask the buyer to trust you even further, by agreeing to a deal in which you are also drafting the documents and holding the deposit. Wouldn't you be a little more than intimidated by this prospect?

A good lawyer is ethically bound to discuss legal rights and obligations of *both* buyer and seller. This reassures a buyer that everything is on the up-and-up. A competent lawyer will provide the credibility and professionalism that you may lack, and thus reassure your buyer. If you enlist professional help, you're unlikely to encounter buyer reluctance to sign on the dotted line.

Buyers for your home should be treated with kid gloves. Don't scare them off with an amateurish attitude.

A good lawyer will be alert to problems early on, and may salvage a deal that you would have botched, because of a lack of experience and knowledge.

DISCUSS PRACTICAL MATTERS

There are many steps to go through before the new owners can move into your house (and you can leave).

Most of us expect a real-estate agent to help us with the nitty-gritty details of moving. You might be pleasantly surprised to know that a competent lawyer will also fill you in on all necessary preparations.

Your lawyer will ask you about the house key, that is how you're planning to ensure the new owners will be able to gain access to the house. Your lawyer will remind you to notify utility companies, in order to guarantee a smooth transition between yourself and the new owners with respect to hydro, phone and utilities. Meters will need to be read, cable disconnected, and so on. He or she will remind you to make final arrangements to ensure your insurance company knows you're selling the home, so that any payment adjustments can be made. For example, taxes and other bills, such as house insurance, are usually paid on an annual basis. If you sell your home in July, and the taxes have been prepaid until December, you'll be entitled to a refund of the difference from the buyer. Alternatively, if you're behind in a tax payment by the time the buyers take possession, you will be obligated to pay the balance owing before you walk away with your profit.

A good lawyer will tie up all the loose ends, so you can get on with your life and forget about the small, but important, details.

If you're thinking about doing these tasks yourself (or hiring a realtor), I urge you to reconsider. Your main objective is to sell your house. If this is done properly, you stand to save thousands of tax-free dollars. When I sold my house, my lawyer's fee amounted to $246.50. I was able to move out of the province and carry on with my life, because my lawyer acted on my behalf in my absence. Remember, a lawyer can replace a realtor, but the converse is not true; a real-estate agent cannot replace a lawyer.

HOW TO RETAIN A LAWYER

I hope that I've persuaded you to hire a lawyer for all your household legal undertakings. The key now is to find someone who is skilled, expedient and will act in your best interest.

I was very fortunate in this regard. I retained the same lawyer through whom I purchased my house. Everything went off smoothly. It wasn't until I purchased a second home in a different city that I realized that not all lawyers are created equal. Believe me, it pays to give this matter serious consideration. I offer the following brief considerations in hiring a lawyer to help you sell your home. If further information is required, there are several books which deal exclusively with this subject.

Availability

Timing is of the essence. Even if a lawyer has a top-notch reputation, if you have to wait a week for an appointment to write up an Offer to Purchase, you may lose a buyer.

Discuss availability at the outset. The decision to buy a home is fragile until a commitment is put in writing. After a potential buyer is found, you should write up the Offer to Purchase within twenty-four hours. My lawyer agreed to see me on short notice, (including meeting with myself and a buyer on a Saturday morning).

Efficiency

Look for a lawyer who works like greased lightning. If someone says to you "I'll get right on it," and a few days go by and you still haven't heard anything, it's time to look for a new lawyer. You want to sell your house and have it done and over with.

Cost

Find out ahead of time how your lawyer's fees are fixed. Some will charge a flat rate, while others charge an hourly fee.

Although all lawyers provide a complete account (Statement of Adjustments) at the end of your transaction, ask whether your lawyer provides a Preliminary Statement of Adjustments. This will give you an advance update on your household assets and liabilities, so you can plan accordingly.

Phone Calls: Often when you're closing a deal you come up with questions. Does your lawyer charge for phone calls? Or, is it next to impossible to get him or her on the phone? Find out ahead of time. It's important to have a lawyer with whom you can communicate. Remember, you don't have a real-estate agent who can intervene on your behalf.

Deals that Fall Through: What if you met with your lawyer to write up an Offer to Purchase and, later on, the deal falls through? What will it cost? This happened to me. My lawyer didn't charge me a cent. He reasoned that, if I didn't make any money, he didn't feel he had earned a fee. Not all lawyers are so generous with their time, but it pays to ask. Remember, setbacks happen, and it isn't a bad strategy to prepare for the worst.

Picture yourself home free. Your house has been sold, and all the legal and business matters concluded. You have no further obligations or responsibilities. Your lawyer has done all the preparations on your behalf. You have all the necessary statements and documents, relieving you of ownership responsibility. Your mortgage has been discharged. Taxes have been adjusted in accordance with the transfer of ownership. Insurance bills and all the expenses that are associated with ownership of the home have been paid in full and cancelled.

The cost of this service? The fee may vary, depending on whether the amount is based on an hourly rate, or a flat rate (usually based on the selling price of the house). This is a pittance, considering the amount of work and expertise required to undertake all the steps necessary to ensure the sale of your home, and the smooth transition from yourself to the buyer.

Let's not forget the importance of a competent lawyer's help in ensuring that your rights are protected, and your obligations fulfilled.

For a real eye opener, compare this fee to a real-estate commission. Suppose you sell your home for $146,000. At a cost of 6% to cover the realtor's fee, you owe the agency a staggering $8,760. Worse yet, you *still* need to hire a lawyer.

Amazing isn't it? Think of what you could buy for $8,760.00 tax-free dollars. As I've stated throughout this book;

> Hiring a real-estate agent should be considered a luxury, not a necessity.
>
> I rest my case.

Chapter Summary

1. A lawyer can replace a real estate agent.

2. A lawyer's fee is a fraction of the real-estate commission.

3. Even if you hire a real-estate agent, you still need to retain a lawyer.

4. Don't attempt to draft the Offer to Purchase, unless you possess expertise in this area. The few dollars you save may cost you the sale of your home.

5. Don't compromise your credibility by holding the deposit.

6. Shop around for a competent lawyer. Consider efficiency, flexibility, and good communication as key factors in your decision.

7. Inquire whether the fee is based on a flat rate, hourly rate, or a percentage of the selling price of the house.

8. No matter what your lawyer charges for a fee, you can be sure you're getting a bargain compared to a real-estate commission.

CHAPTER 17

THE LIVING END

You've done it. The house is sold. Before you leave, ensure the items covered in the following checklist are completed, thus assuring a smooth, courteous transition for both yourself and your buyer.

1. Cancel or notify all services—hydro, gas or oil company, cable, phone, newspaper, mail, etcetera.

2. Notify insurance companies.

3. Leave all fixtures that are attached to the house (including track lighting, dimmer switches and rheostats). This is a legal requirement.

4. Leave your forwarding address for the new owners.

5. Be thoughtful. Leave the house clean. If you're including household items with the sale, such as fridge or stove, leave these clean and in working order.

6. Review the conditions of the offer of sale. Make sure you leave all items specified in the terms of the agreement.

7. Open the champagne. Celebrate! You've earned it!!!